# Invitation
## *to the* Psalms

SECOND EDITION

# Invitation
## *to the* Psalms

### A READER'S GUIDE
### FOR DISCOVERY AND ENGAGEMENT

## ROLF A. JACOBSON
## AND KARL N. JACOBSON

Baker Academic

*a division of Baker Publishing Group*

Grand Rapids, Michigan

© 2013, 2024 by Rolf A. Jacobson and Karl Jacobson

Published by Baker Academic
a division of Baker Publishing Group
Grand Rapids, Michigan
BakerAcademic.com

Printed in the United States of America

Library of Congress Cataloging-in-Publication Data
Names: Jacobson, Rolf A., author. | Jacobson, Karl N., 1969– author.
Title: Invitation to the psalms : a reader's guide for discovery and engagement / Rolf A. Jacobson, Karl N. Jacobson.
Description: Second edition. | Grand Rapids, Michigan : Baker Academic, a division of Baker Publishing Group, [2024] | Includes bibliographical references and index.
Identifiers: LCCN 2024010428 | ISBN 9781540967978 (paperback) | ISBN 9781540968319 (casebound) | ISBN 9781493447565 (ebook) | ISBN 9781493447572 (pdf)
Subjects: LCSH: Bible. Psalms—Textbooks.
Classification: LCC BS1451 .J33 2024 | DDC 223/.2007—dc23/eng/20240329
LC record available at https://lccn.loc.gov/2024010428

Cover design by Paula Gibson
Cover art: *Rain Clouds and Sea* by Frederick Judd Waugh, Christie's Images Ltd/Superstock

Baker Publishing Group publications use paper produced from sustainable forestry practices and postconsumer waste whenever possible.

24   25   26   27   28   29   30        7   6   5   4   3   2   1

*To Anne and Karen*

# Contents

# Introduction

Let the words of my mouth and the meditation of my heart
  be acceptable to you,
  O Lᴏʀᴅ, my rock and my redeemer.

—Psalm 19:14

These are the final words of Psalm 19. In the psalm itself, the words are appended as a parting prayer, a faithful wish that God might find the psalmist's poem to be an acceptable offering. In some Christian traditions, these words have often been prayed at the start of the sermon, in the hopes that the preacher's words might matter—if only in some small way.

The words also seemed a fitting way to begin this book because it is meant more as an invitation to read the psalms than as an analysis of what they say or mean. *The psalms are meant to be read; they are meant to be experienced.* Analysis of poetry is helpful and important—but only if that analysis serves to assist the reader to enter into a poem with greater sensitivity. Analysis is a *servant.* A competent reader analyzes poetry so that the poetry itself can speak more profoundly. This is true of all poetry—and it is especially true of the psalms, which are the poetry of Christian and Jewish faith.

In his influential essay *How Does a Poem Mean?*, John Ciardi writes, "Analysis is never in any sense a substitute for the poem. The best any analysis can do is to prepare the reader to enter the poem more perceptively."[1] He adds

1. John Ciardi, *How Does a Poem Mean?* (New York: Houghton Mifflin, 1959), 663.

1

that the concern of poetry "is not to arrive at a definition and to close the book, but to arrive at an experience."[2] For that reason, according to Ciardi, the reader of poetry should not ask "What does a poem mean?" but rather "How does a poem mean?" Poetry is not merely expressive; *it is expression*. Poems, that is, do not merely talk about love or passion or emotion: they are the very sound of love, of passion, of emotion.

Because the psalms are the poetry of faith, they are not meant to be studied; they are meant to be read. The prayers of the Psalter are meant to be prayed. The songs of the Psalter are meant to be sung. The lessons of the Psalter are meant to be lived. The angry psalms are meant to be shouted. The meditations are meant to be meditated on. When it comes to Psalm 23, the most well-known of all psalms, it is meant not as a lesson for a teacher to commend to a student but as a prayer to be prayed:

> The LORD is my shepherd, I shall not want.
>     He makes me lie down in green pastures;
> he leads me beside still waters;
>     he restores my soul.
> He leads me in right paths,
>     for his name's sake. (vv. 1–3)

The psalm does not just describe trust; *it is an expression of trust*. When the faithful follower prays the psalm, the psalm does not merely express how the pray-er feels. Rather, through praying the psalm the pray-er comes to trust.

If there is any value in learning about the psalms, it is just this: by learning about the psalms the students may learn to read, pray, sing, shout, chant, and wonder the psalms.

This book is an invitation to do just that. The information that is offered here is not meant as a replacement for the psalms—in the way that the Cliffs-Notes condensed study guides are meant as replacements for actually reading various works of literature. Rather, the analysis offered here may be likened to the sort of information that is offered in a tour-guide pamphlet. The goal is to familiarize the reader with the landscape of the Psalter so that the reader will be set loose to explore the Psalter and roam widely among its poems. Billy Collins, in the famous poem "Introduction to Poetry,"[3] poetically scores this point:

2. Ciardi, *How Does a Poem Mean?*, 666.
3. Billy Collins, "Introduction to Poetry," in *The Apple That Astonished Paris: Poems* (Fayetteville: University of Arkansas Press, 1988), 58. Copyright © 1988 by Billy Collins. Reprinted with the permission of The Permissions Company, Inc., on behalf of the University of Arkansas Press, www.uapress.com.

### Introduction to Poetry

I ask them to take a poem
and hold it up to the light
like a color slide

or press an ear against its hive.

I say drop a mouse into a poem
and watch him probe his way out,

or walk inside the poem's room
and feel the walls for a light switch.

I want them to waterski
across the surface of a poem
waving at the author's name on the shore.

But all they want to do
is tie the poem to a chair with rope
and torture a confession out of it.

They begin beating it with a hose
to find out what it really means.

To reduce a poem to its meaning or to summarize its message is to "torture a confession out of it" in order "to find out what it really means." To read a psalm is, in Collins's marvelous language, "to waterski across [its] surface," to "press an ear against its hive," to "hold it up to the light." For that reason we use a great many examples from the psalms themselves. Writing this book, when we had to make a decision between quoting more of a psalm or less of a psalm, our motto was "more is better."

The intended audience for this book is the interested nonspecialist student—the student who does not read biblical Hebrew or who has only passing familiarity with Hebrew. For the most part, we have avoided arcane topics of debates of psalms interpretation—the sort of sticky-wicket technical issues that only the hyperspecialist would care about. Similarly, we have avoided lengthy footnotes filled with dizzying displays of our dazzling grasp of the secondary literature. In place of many notes, at the end of each chapter we provide short bibliographies that list appropriate further reading for beginning students of the psalms.

We have chosen to concentrate on the most accessible features of the psalms—their poetry (chap. 1), the basic genres of psalms (chaps. 2–3), the voice of "the psalmist" (chap. 4), the metaphors of the psalms (chap. 5), and the theology of the psalms (chap. 7).

For the second edition, we have also added a chapter discussing recent approaches to the psalms that focus on the shape and organization of the book of Psalms as a whole (chap. 6). We have also edited each chapter and added sidebars to the chapters highlighting how the psalms have been heard and used in popular culture.

We begin with poetry for two reasons: First, because the rhythms of Hebrew poetry are foreign to most English readers. Second, because we believe that the psalms are poetry. Although many have tried to do so, one cannot separate the poetic form of the psalm from the intellectual content of the psalm. To try to do so is like trying to separate the wet from water, or the heat from fire. We then proceed with familiarizing the reader with the basic genres of the psalms based on the assumption that words have meaning only in context, and the genres of the psalms offer the primary literary context in which the words of the psalms make sense. We then proceed by introducing the reader to the living "voice of the psalmist," to a consideration of the rich metaphorical life of these poems, to an interpretation of the God of the psalms, and finally to the shape of the Psalter.

When reading the psalms, the reader will face an entire set of minor, technical irritations. One of these is that the enumeration of the psalms and especially of the verses of the psalms varies from one version to another. There are two widely used systems for numbering the psalms, one based on the Hebrew text (the so-called Masoretic Text [MT]) and one based on an ancient translation of the psalms into Greek (the so-called Septuagint, or "Old Greek" version of the Old Testament [LXX or OG]). The order of the psalms in these two systems is the same, but the enumeration differs slightly:

| Hebrew (MT) | Greek (LXX or OG) |
| --- | --- |
| 1–8 | 1–8 |
| 9–10 | 9 |
| 11–113 | 10–112 |
| 114–115 | 113 |
| 116:1–9 | 114 |
| 116:10–19 | 115 |
| 117–146 | 116–145 |
| 147:1–11 | 146 |
| 147:12–20 | 147 |
| 148–150 | 148–150 |

In addition, there are two basic systems for enumerating the verses of the psalms. In general, the two systems treat the superscriptions of the psalms differently. The term "superscription" refers to information included at the start of some psalms, such as "A Psalm of David" (Ps. 23) or "To the leader: according to The Deer of the Dawn. A Psalm of David" (Ps. 22). Beginning with the King James Version (KJV), most English versions, including the New Revised Standard Version (NRSV) and the New International Version (NIV), have not numbered the superscription but have counted as "verse 1" whatever follows the superscription. Other English versions, such as the New Jewish Publication Society version (NJPS), do count the superscription as verse 1 and then continue enumerating. In this book we join the majority of English versions by following the Hebrew (MT) textual tradition when it comes to both numbering the psalms and *not* counting the superscriptions as verse 1.

Finally, two words of thanks. First, to Rolf's daughter Ingrid, who read through the first edition and offered feedback both on what worked well in that edition and also on what we might change or add. Thank you, Ingrid. Second, to our older sisters, Anne and Karen. Psalm 133:1 says, "How very good and pleasant it is when kindred live together in unity!" It may be "good and pleasant," but when the four of us were kids, living "together in unity" may not have seemed to our parents like a daily experience. In this, as in many things, getting older is a blessing. We still look up to you, continue to learn from your wisdom, and deeply respect you. Two little brothers could not have asked for two more marvelous sisters. We love you. This book is dedicated to you.

PS: When we dedicated the first edition to our sisters, we joked that "Mom loves us best." Since then, in December 2020, our mom died. She had suffered a stroke in July of that year. Her final months unfolded during the COVID lockdown; it wasn't always fun. We prayed many psalms during those months. Mom died late one December evening—in her bedroom, with our dad at her side. He reported to us, "I prayed Psalm 23 and then the Lord's Prayer. Sometime between the start of the one and the end of the next, your mother died." That was fitting in so many ways. With gratitude, we join our sisters and father in remembering the words of Psalm 23: "Even though I walk through the valley of the shadow of death, I shall fear no evil; for you are with me." This book is indeed for our sisters, with whom we shared such wonderful parents. Mom and Dad were our first Scripture teachers. They taught us to love God (always) and each other (most of the time), and they offered us each an invitation to the psalms.

ONE

# Why Is My Bible Repeating Itself?

*Learning to Understand Hebrew Poetry*

## Introducing Hebrew Poetry

The biblical book of Psalms is, first and foremost, a collection of Hebrew poetry. If a reader sets out to understand the psalms—or even to understand a single one of the psalms—that reader must take into account the central reality that the psalms are Hebrew poetry. Why? Because reading is a "logical" exercise—in the sense that words, phrases, and sentences are put together according to principles that are governed by a logic. You cannot understand what the words, phrases, and sentences are trying to communicate if you do not understand that governing logic. Poetry as a whole is a type of language that has a different governing logic from other types of writing. And Hebrew poetry, in particular, has an even more specifically different set of governing logic.

An example may help. Mathematical equations are basically sentences that use numerical and mathematical symbols rather than words to communicate. Imagine that you are given the task of understanding what the following mathematical equation (sentence) is trying to communicate:

$$2 + 2 = 4$$

The meaning is transparently clear, right? Before you answer yes, imagine that you do not understand what numbers are or how they work. Imagine that you do not understand that the symbol "2" represents the numerical concept of two. Or that the symbol "4" represents the numerical concept of four. Furthermore, imagine that you do not understand that the symbols "+" and "=" stand for the concepts of adding and totaling, respectively. A reader who does not understand these things could, of course, not understand even the simplest equation. The reason for this is that the basic building block of mathematical equations is a signification system in which 2 = two, + = addition, and so on. A reader who does not understand that system cannot understand the longer "sentences" that are created when various elements such as 2, 4, +, and = are put together. But a reader who does understand these basic building blocks and how they work can understand even complex mathematical sentences, like the quadratic formula: $ax^2 + bx + c = 0$ (where $a \neq 0$). Now that we've exceeded what we know about math, let us return to Hebrew poetry.

Just as numerical and mathematical symbols are the building blocks of mathematical sentences, Hebrew poetry is the basic building block of the biblical psalms. In order to understand the overall message that a psalm is trying to communicate, it is helpful (perhaps even "necessary") to know some basic elements about the governing logic of Hebrew poetry. When a reader does not understand the basic features of Hebrew poetry and how they work, that reader will find it almost impossible to read and understand even the simplest lines from the psalms, such as, "The LORD is in his holy temple; the LORD's throne is in heaven" (Ps. 11:4). But a reader who does understand these basic building blocks can read *and understand* even complex psalms.

The thesis of this chapter is that if readers of the psalms will take the time to understand the basic conventions and features of Hebrew poetry, they will be in a far better position to understand the witness of the psalms—to "waterski across the surface" of a psalm. In this chapter we explain and illustrate some of these central conventions, beginning with a concept that is usually called parallelism.

## Understanding Parallelism

If you have ever read the psalms, you may wonder why your Bible is repeating itself. Consider these four examples from the psalms:

[A]  what are human beings that you are mindful of them,
[B]      mortals that you care for them? (8:4)

[A]  I will give thanks to you, O LORD, among the peoples,
[B]       I will sing praises to you among the nations. (108:3)

[A]  O God, do not keep silence;
[B]       do not hold your peace or be still, O God! (83:1)

[A]  You forgave the iniquity of your people;
[B]       you pardoned all of their sin. (85:2)

In each of these examples, the second line is very similar to the first line. One could almost—almost, but not quite—say that the second line simply repeats the sentiments of the first line. One could *almost* say that the second lines are basically *synonyms* for the meanings of the first lines.

The four examples above nicely illustrate the basic building block of Hebrew poetry, which scholars call *parallelism*. The term "parallelism" was coined by a scholar named Christian Schöttgen in 1733, who described "the linking of entire sentences, several words or clauses of sentences . . . in a kind of parallelism."[1] The term was made famous by Robert Lowth, a bishop of the Church of England, who in 1753 published a very influential study of biblical poetry.[2] Parallelism can be defined most briefly as *the repetition of elements within a grammatical unit.*

The four examples above all show repetition in the "grammatical unit" that we are calling a *line* (above, the lines are each marked either as A or as B). But note that scholars also use several terms to demark this unit of text, including "colon" (plural: cola) and stich (plural: stichoi). We will use the term "verse" for a unit of poetry normally made up of two or more lines—above, there are four "verses" of poetry; each verse is made up of two lines.

Within biblical scholarship, most interpreters focus on parallelism between lines, but parallelism occurs at many different levels in Hebrew poetry: within lines, between lines, between verses, between entire sections, and between psalms.

### Parallelism Can Occur within a Line of Hebrew Poetry

[A]  The LORD is my light and my salvation. (27:1a)

[A]  The LORD is gracious and merciful,
[B]       slow to anger and abounding in steadfast love. (145:8)

---

1. Claus Seybold, *Studien zu Sprache und Stil der Psalmen* (Berlin: de Gruyter, 2010), 8. Thanks to Seybold for this reference: Christian Schöttgen, *Horae hebraicae et talmudicae* (Dresden: Hekel, 1733), 1:1252; cf. https://www.catholic.com/encyclopedia/parallelism.
2. Robert Lowth, *De sacra poesi Hebraeorum* [Lectures on the Sacred Poetry of the Hebrews] (Oxford: Clarendon, 1753).

In these two examples there are parallel sets of words to describe God *within each line.* In the first example, "my light" is used *in parallel* with "my salvation." In the second example, parallelism occurs within both lines. In line A of Psalm 145:8, the single word "gracious" is used in parallel with the single word "merciful," while in the second line the phrase "slow to anger" is used in parallel with the phrase "abounding in steadfast love." Thus, parallelism can occur within a line of Hebrew poetry. Now it is your turn to try it. Finish these two lines of poetry and make sure that you include some parallelism within the lines:

Praise the Lord with _____.

I will sing of _____.

If you want to see how an ancient poet handled the same lines that you were given, you can check out Psalm 150:3–4a and 101:1a. But remember, the purpose of this little exercise is not to try to "get it right" by guessing exactly what the ancient poet wrote. Rather, the purpose is to "get it right" by showing that you are beginning to understand what parallelism is and how it works.

### Parallelism Can Occur between Lines of Hebrew Poetry

[A]  Where can I go from your spirit?
[B]     Or where can I flee from your presence? (139:7)

[A]  The Lord is gracious and merciful,
[B]     slow to anger and abounding in steadfast love. (145:8)

[A]  Fortunate is the one who does not walk in the advice of the wicked,
[B]     who does not stand on the path that sinners tread,
[C]     who does not sit in the seat of scoffers. (1:1 AT)

In these three examples the repetition is between lines. Notice especially that in the first two examples, there are two lines in parallel with each other, but that in the third example three lines are in parallel with each other. This tripartite parallelism is less common than the bipartite parallelism, but it occurs frequently enough that readers should be aware of it. This *line-level parallelism* is the part of Hebrew poetry that has been studied the most. Indeed, a great deal of ink has been spilled by scholars arguing with one another over how best to describe it.

As you will see in the next paragraph, some scholars have tried to categorize the many and various ways in which the A lines of Hebrew poetry are parallel to the B lines. Like an extremely organized person who lines up all of the spices alphabetically in the cupboard, scholars have tried to organize how Hebrew poetry works. But, like the spices in the cupboard, all of these attempts work for a while and then sort of crash to the ground. After all, do you alphabetize "Crushed Red Pepper" under C, R, or P? And what about "Lemon Pepper," which is not really lemon or pepper? Our point is that the impulse to categorize things is usually helpful, but achieving a perfect or complete categorization is not always possible. We believe that this is the case with Hebrew poetry.

Bishop Lowth got the whole categorizing thing going when he asserted that there are three types of parallelism:

- *synonymous parallelism*, in which the second line basically says the same thing as the first line;
- *antithetical parallelism*, in which the second line basically says the opposite of the first line; and
- *synthetic parallelism*, in which the second line says neither the same thing as nor the opposite of the first line.

The obvious problem with Lowth's categories is that if you need a catchall category such as "synthetic parallelism" to fit in everything that does not fit into your other categories, maybe there is a problem with your categories. Or, as we maintain, maybe the real problem is that *there is a problem with trying to categorize art*!

The real danger in trying to categorize the way parallelism works, however, is not that such categorization cannot be done but that such categorization might lead readers to think that they have adequately analyzed the poetry of a psalm once they have assigned a label such as "synthetic parallelism" to a verse. The truly unhelpful dimension about this categorizing approach, then, is that it limits the imagination of readers. It exposes readers to a superficial level of analysis, which can prevent them from engaging in the deeper levels of meaning in the poem. It presents readers with a way of labeling the poetry but does not show them how to digest the poetry. As we wrote in the introduction, the purpose of analysis is to help a reader enter a psalm.

So, for now, all you need to know is this: in Hebrew poetry, parallelism occurs between lines of poetry. Once you know that, the challenge of reading Hebrew poetry is not to try to assign a label to the poetry—such as *synthetic parallelism*—but is rather to understand what the poetry is meaning. Or, to use a metaphor that is almost poetic, the joy of reading Hebrew poetry comes from getting the "feel" of parallelism and learning to "enjoy the ride."

Once again, it is now your turn. We will give you the first line of a real psalm and let you write a line that would work in parallel with it:

Great is the LORD and greatly to be praised,

_____ .

Hear, O daughter, consider and incline your ear,

_____ .

Have mercy on me, O God,

_____ .

If you want to compare your poetry with that of the ancient Hebrew poets, you can read Psalms 48:1; 45:10; and 51:1. But remember, you are not "right" if you write exactly what the psalmist did; you are right if you are beginning to understand the rhythms of Hebrew poetry.

### Parallelism Can Occur between Verses of Hebrew Poetry

Consider these examples from the psalms:

[A] O LORD, how many are my foes!
[B]     Many are rising against me;
[C] many are saying to me,
[D]     "There is no help for you in God." (3:1–2)

[E] If I ascend to heaven, you are there;
[F]     if I make my bed in Sheol, you are there.
[G] If I take the wings of the morning
[H]     and settle at the farthest limits of the sea (139:8–9)

In these two examples, parallelism occurs between verses. In the example from Psalm 3, there are two verses made up of four lines. Basically, the second verse as a whole is in parallel to the first verse. Notice that line B and line C are very similar, both having this form: "Many are _____ing __ me." This very similar element in each verse thus becomes like a hinge in the middle of the two verses, around which the two verses as a whole swing. It may be easier to see how the two verses function in parallel to each other if the verses are laid out like this:

A O LORD, how many are my foes!
　B Many are rising against me;
　B′ Many are saying to me,
A′ "There is no help for you in God."

In the example from Psalm 139, parallelism again occurs between the two verses. Notice that the first line of each verse begins with a conditional "if" statement.[3] But notice also that in the first lines of each verse (E and G), there is a statement that is related both to flying and to the sky: "ascend to heaven" in line E and "take the wings of the morning" in line G. Then in the second lines of each verse (F and H), there are statements related both to a sedentary bodily position and to what the ancient Hebrews would have recognized as a netherworld: "make my bed in Sheol" and "dwell at the farthest limits of the sea" (Sheol was the place of the dead, where people go after life ends; the sea was the place of chaos, where the Canaanite god of the dead reigned). Thus, we could diagram the way these two verses function in parallel with one another as something like this:

> If . . . reference to flying . . . reference to the sky
>> Reference to sedentary act . . . reference to netherworld
> If . . . reference to flying . . . reference to the sky
>> Reference to sedentary act . . . reference to netherworld

And once again, now it is your turn. You are given two full verses of Hebrew poetry. Write two more verses that will function in parallel to these two verses:

> The sea looked and fled;
>> Jordan turned back.
> The mountains skipped like rams,
>> the hills like lambs.

_____

_____

_____

_____

If you want to compare your parallelism with that of the ancient psalm writer, read Psalm 114.

3. In the Hebrew of Ps. 139, there is only one instance of the conditional particle that we translate as "if." This occurs at the start of v. 8. But in the syntax of Hebrew poetry, it is not necessary to repeat the "if" at the start of each phrase or line. The particle governs each of the lines, even though it occurs only at the start of the first line of a series of parallels. Scholars refer to this syntactical phenomenon as the particle doing "double duty"—in this case triple duty since the particle governs lines E, F, and G.

### *Parallelism Can Occur between Entire Sections of a Psalm*

In addition to occurring within a line, between lines, and between verses of poetry, parallelism can occur between entire sections of a psalm. Consider the way in which Psalms 42–43 (these two separately numbered poems actually form one psalm) have a refrain that occurs three times, basically creating three parallel sections of the psalm:

| Psalm 42 A | Psalm 42 B | Psalm 43 |
|---|---|---|
| As a deer longs for flowing streams, so my soul longs for you, O God. My soul thirsts for God, for the living God. When shall I come and behold the face of God? My tears have been my food day and night, while people say to me continually, "Where is your God?" These things I remember, as I pour out my soul: how I went with the throng, and led them in procession to the house of God, with glad shouts and songs of thanksgiving, a multitude keeping festival. | My soul is cast down within me; therefore I remember you from the land of Jordan and of Herman, from Mount Mizar. Deep calls to deep at the thunder of your cataracts; all your waves and your billows have gone over me. By day the LORD commands his steadfast love, and at night his song is with me, a prayer to the God of my life. I say to God, my rock, "Why have you forgotten me? Why must I walk about mournfully because the enemy oppresses me?" As with a deadly wound in my body, my adversaries taunt me, while they say to me continually, "Where is your God?" | Vindicate me, O God, and defend my cause against an ungodly people; from those who are deceitful and unjust deliver me! For you are the God in whom I take refuge; why have you cast me off? Why must I walk about mournfully because of the oppression of the enemy? O send out your light and your truth; let them lead me; let them bring me to your holy hill and to your dwelling. Then I will go to the altar of God, to God my exceeding joy; and I will praise you with the harp, O God, my God. |
| Why are you cast down, O my soul, and why are you disquieted within me? Hope in God; for I shall again praise him, my help and my God. | Why are you cast down, O my soul, and why are you disquieted within me? Hope in God; for I shall again praise him, my help and my God. | Why are you cast down, O my soul, and why are you disquieted within me? Hope in God; for I shall again praise him, my help and my God. |

We arranged Psalms 42 and 43 in three columns to illustrate that this psalm has three parallel "panes." Each section ends with the refrain that begins, "Why are you cast down, O my soul?" This psalm illustrates that parallelism can occur between entire sections of psalms. Other psalms in which this form of parallelism occurs are Psalms 107 and 119.

### Parallelism Can Occur between Two Psalms

Parallelism also occurs between psalms. That is, the editors who collected all 150 psalms and arranged them into the book of Psalms intentionally placed certain psalms next to each other. In this final arrangement, the two psalms may be read "in parallel" with each other. This type of arrangement, sometimes called "twin psalms," occurs in many places, such as Psalms 1–2; 103–104; 105–106; and 113–114. But perhaps the clearest example of this is found in the twin psalms 111–112 (see below). Both psalms are alphabetic acrostic psalms: each line of these psalms begins with a successive letter of the Hebrew alphabet. Both psalms begin with the call, "Praise the Lord!" Psalm 111 is about God and God's ways, whereas Psalm 112 is about those who follow God and who follow God's ways. One commentator has titled these two psalms "The ABCs of Theology" and "The ABCs of Anthropology."[4]

---

## PSALM III

[1] Praise the Lord!
I will give thanks to the Lord with my whole heart,
    in the company of the upright, in the congregation.
[2] Great are the works of the Lord,
    studied by all who delight in them.
[3] Full of honor and majesty is his work,
    and his righteousness endures forever.
[4] He has gained renown by his wonderful deeds;
    the Lord is gracious and merciful.
[5] He provides food for those who fear him;
    he is ever mindful of his covenant.
[6] He has shown his people the power of his works,
    in giving them the heritage of the nations.
[7] The works of his hands are faithful and just;
    all his precepts are trustworthy.
[8] They are established forever and ever,
    to be performed with faithfulness and uprightness.
[9] He sent redemption to his people;
    he has commanded his covenant forever.
    Holy and awesome is his name.
[10] The fear of the Lord is the beginning of wisdom;
    all those who practice it have a good understanding.
    His praise endures forever.

---

4. James Limburg, *Psalms* (Louisville: Westminster John Knox, 2000), 381–87.

## PSALM 112

¹Praise the LORD!
  Happy are those who fear the LORD,
    who greatly delight in his commandments.
² Their descendants will be mighty in the land;
    the generation of the upright will be blessed.
³ Wealth and riches are in their houses,
    and their righteousness endures forever.
⁴ They rise in the darkness as a light for the upright;
    they are gracious, merciful, and righteous.
⁵ It is well with those who deal generously and lend,
    who conduct their affairs with justice.
⁶ For the righteous will never be moved;
    they will be remembered forever.
⁷ They are not afraid of evil tidings;
    their hearts are firm, secure in the LORD.
⁸ Their hearts are steady, they will not be afraid;
    in the end they will look in triumph on their foes.
⁹ They have distributed freely, they have given to the poor;
    their righteousness endures forever;
    their horn is exalted in honor.
¹⁰ The wicked see it and are angry;
    they gnash their teeth and melt away;
    the desire of the wicked comes to nothing.

### Echoing and Extending: The Building Blocks of Parallelism

There is one more aspect of biblical parallelism that we believe is useful for the beginning reader of the psalms to know. Up to this point, the focus has been on identifying what parallelism is and where it occurs. Now we wish to change the focus to *how* parallelism is built, to help the beginning reader develop an understanding of what the basic building blocks of parallelism are.

The twin concepts of "echoing" and "extending" provide a helpful set of lenses through which one can understand the building blocks of parallelism. *In most parallelism, the second element of the parallelism either echoes or extends the first element—and usually it does both.*

*Echoing.* We use the term "echo" to describe how a word, phrase, or sentence responds in a ping-pong-like manner to a word, phrase, or sentence. In the following set of words, the secondary word echoes the first in some manner.

| day ↔ night | day ↔ sunrise | day ↔ month | day ↔ days |
| love ↔ hate | love ↔ mercy | love ↔ beloved | love ↔ forgive |
| Jerusalem ↔ temple | Jerusalem ↔ Judah | Jerusalem ↔ David | |
| I ↔ my soul | I ↔ you | I ↔ my bones | I ↔ they |
| sing ↔ praise | sing ↔ be silent | sing ↔ new song | |

Each of these pairs of words can be said to be functioning in an echoing manner. The echo does not have to be noun for noun or verb for verb. Nor does the echo need to be a synonym or an antonym. The second word may be a synonym, an antonym, a complementary concept, a plural form of the first, a smaller subset or part of the first word, a noun that corresponds with a verb, and so on. There are an almost infinite number of ways that the second term can echo the first.

The concept of echoing also takes place with phrases. Consider the following set of corresponding phrases, each of which is taken from a biblical psalm:

| |
| --- |
| for a moment ↔ for a lifetime |
| up from Sheol ↔ down to the pit |
| sin with my tongue ↔ muzzle on my mouth |
| I shall be clean ↔ I shall be whiter than snow |
| up to my neck ↔ no foothold |
| lift your horn on high ↔ speak with insolent neck |

Notice that sometimes the echoing phrases take almost an identical form, while other times the echoing interplay takes a more free form. But echoing is only one of the two basic building blocks of Hebrew parallelism; a second one, which we call extending, also exists.

*Extending.* We use the term "extend" to describe how a word, phrase, or sentence can *build on and continue* the thought of a previous word, phrase, or sentence. Although parallel poetic elements that "echo" take the energy from the first element and fire it back, parallel poetic elements that "extend" take the energy from the first element and give it a boost forward. Whereas we described "echoing" as being like a ping-pong game, "extending" is like a relay race: the first element passes the baton to the second, which carries it forward. Extending parallelism takes the baton and keeps going. Consider these sets of words and phrases:

| |
| --- |
| red ↔ wagon |
| fast ↔ reader |

| | |
|---|---|
| quickly ↔ descend | |
| like trees planted by streams of water ↔ which yield their fruit in due season | |
| the decrees of the LORD are sure ↔ making wise the simple | |
| Who can detect their errors? ↔ Clear me from hidden faults. | |

In each of these examples, the secondary element takes the ball from the primary element and runs with it. The secondary element does not merely echo back at the primary element but also picks up the concept and explores a direction in which it might go.

*Echoing and extending.* In Hebrew parallelism, the norm is that the secondary element is usually *both echoing and extending* the primary element in some fashion. Do not misunderstand! Do not reduce parallelism to either echoing or extending! Normally there are features of both echoing and extending going on. Consider a few examples:

> Let the redeemed of the LORD say so,
>> those he redeemed from trouble. (107:2)

Notice that the second phrase echoes the first phrase by repeating God's action of redeeming: "redeemed of the LORD" ↔ "those he redeemed." But notice that it also extends by defining more precisely what God redeemed the people from: "redeemed" ↔ "from trouble." Here is another example:

> The days of our life are seventy years,
>> or perhaps eighty, if we are strong. (90:10a)

The second phrase both echoes the statement of the first phrase by repeating a number: "seventy" ↔ "eighty." Yet it also extends the thought of the first phrase by applying a condition to the statement: "seventy years" ↔ "eighty, *if we are strong.*" And one more example:

> The dullard cannot know,
>> the stupid cannot understand this. (92:6)

The second phrase echoes the concept that there are some who cannot comprehend: "The dullard cannot know" ↔ "the stupid cannot understand." But it then defines precisely what the stupid cannot understand: "cannot know" ↔ "cannot understand *this.*" Next the psalm continues to "extend" as it goes on to describe precisely what the stupid do not understand. If you want to know what the stupid cannot understand, you will need to read the rest of Psalm 92.

Once again, we wish to stress a basic point: the purpose of learning about the "echoing" and "extending" aspect of Hebrew poetry is not to label the various elements of the poetry and then close off interpretation. Rather, the purpose is for the beginning interpreter to learn the basic rhythm of the poetry so that one can ride along on the crest of the poetry, so to speak.

## Understanding Poetic Structure and Development

Earlier in this chapter, we introduced psalms as forms of human expression that are governed by certain sets of logic. A first set of logic that governs the psalms (as well as all other Hebrew poetry) is the logic of parallelism. A second set of logic that governs the biblical psalms is a logic of *structure* and *development*. Most forms of human communication are governed by some logic of structure. For example, telephone conversations are governed by the logic of

alert → greeting → identification → communication

The phone rings or buzzes (alert). A person answers and says, "Hello" (greeting). The caller says something like, "Hi, it's Mom calling" (identification). Then the call continues (communication). Another example is a three-part joke. Many jokes have three parts (example, "Three fonts— Courier, Times New Roman, and Arial—walk into a bar, and they each order a beer . . ."). The first two parts set the pattern, and the third deviates from the pattern: this deviation is intended to be funny. For example: ". . . the bartender served the first two, but said to the third, 'Hey, we don't serve your type in here.'" (Remember that we said this joke is *intended* to be funny. There are no guarantees.) The point is that many forms of communication depend on structure to communicate meaning. Oftentimes humans are so deeply familiar with a form of communication that they do not ever realize that there is an apparent structure. But when a reader is trying to understand and interpret a new form of communication, paying attention to structure and development can be very helpful.

### First Example: Question-Answer Structure

Paying careful attention to structure is important when learning to read the psalms. Like other forms of communication, the psalms have structure and develop according to certain sets of logic. But rather than all of the psalms sharing one structure, each of the psalms tends to have its own unique structure and tends to develop according to its individual logic. And quite often, unlocking the logic of a psalm's structure is the key to unpacking its meaning. And the more deeply one can understand the structure of a psalm, the more complete one's understanding of a psalm will be. Consider the following example.

### Psalm 121

¹ I lift up my eyes to the hills—
    from where will my help come?
² My help comes from the LORD,
    who made heaven and earth.

³ He will not let your foot be moved;
    Your keeper will not slumber.
⁴ Israel's keeper
    will not slumber or sleep.

⁵ The LORD is your keeper;
    the LORD is your shade at your right hand.
⁶ The sun shall not strike you by day,
    nor the moon by night.

⁷ The LORD will keep you from all evil;
    he will keep your life.
⁸ The LORD will keep your going out and your coming in
    from this time on and forevermore. (AT)

At the most basic level, the structure of the psalm is *question* and *answer*. The first verse poses a question: "I lift up my eyes to the hills—from where will my help come?" The rest of the psalm provides an answer: "My help comes from the LORD, who made heaven and earth." So, in terms of understanding the meaning of the psalm, this basic level of structure helps one understand its basic message. One might sum it up this way: Psalm 121 asks the question, *"To whom can a person turn for help?"* Then it provides its own answer: *"One can turn to the LORD, who 'keeps' those who 'come and go' as they journey."*

Notice that there is a second level of structure to this psalm. Verses 1–2 are spoken in the first person: "I lift . . . my eyes . . . my help . . . my help . . ." The rest of the psalm (vv. 3–8) is spoken in the second person: "He will not let your foot . . . he who keeps you . . . your keeper . . . your shade . . . your life . . . your going out and your coming in . . ." So, in terms of understanding the meaning of the psalm, this second level of structure helps one understand its message slightly more deeply. One might sum it up as follows: In Psalm 121, two speakers converse. A first speaker asks a question and provides an initial answer: *"Who do I turn to for help? I turn to the* Lord *for help."* Then a second speaker responds with words of promise: *"The* Lord *will keep you safe as you travel."* Further, notice that this second level of structure invites some further questions. These questions include (1) Who are these two speakers? (2) What is the occasion upon which they spoke? Scholars (of course) disagree about the answers to these questions. Based on a close reading of the poem, the most widely accepted likely interpretation is this: A person about to set out on a journey spoke verses 1–2 (*I am about to leave. Who will help me as I travel through those distant hills? The* Lord, *who made those hills and everything else that exists*). A second person then speaks (*As you travel, the* Lord, *who guides and protects our entire people, will guide and protect you on your journey until you return*).

But there is also a third and even more complex level to the structure of Psalm 121. Notice that in verses 3–8, the word "keep" occurs six times: three times as "keeper" in verses 3–5 and three times as "will keep" in verses 7–8. In the middle of these repetitions, verses 5b–6—with references to "shade," "sun," and "moon"—sit at the "center" of this part of the psalm. Furthermore, this section of the psalm employs the personal name of God ("the Lord" in English translation, "Yahweh" in Hebrew) four times. These occurrences of the divine name also are balanced around verses 5b–6: two occur before the center section, and two occur after it:

A   He will not let your foot be moved;
  Your *keeper* will not slumber.
  B   Israel's *keeper*
    will not slumber or sleep.
    C   The Lord is your *keeper*;
      the Lord is your shade at your right hand.
      D   The sun shall not strike you by day,
        nor the moon by night.
    C′  The Lord *will keep* you from all evil;
  B′  he *will keep* your life.
A′  The Lord *will keep* your going out and your coming in
  from this time on and forevermore.

The carefully crafted structure of verses 3–8 suggests that the psalm is far from an off-the-cuff exchange. Rather, it is a carefully crafted liturgy, most likely designed for repeated use by a community. The formal nature of the liturgy helps the reader speculate a little further on the identification of the second speaker. Most likely this second speaker is either a priest or some other community elder, who speaks formal words of blessing on a traveler who is departing on a journey.

As mentioned above, each psalm has its own unique structure. But there are common features to look for as well as common patterns to be aware of. Psalm 121, as just noted, opens with a question, and then the rest of the psalm is effectively a response to that question. Other psalms share that structure. Notice how Psalm 115 unfolds:

> Not to us, O LORD, not to us, but to your name give glory,
>     for the sake of your steadfast love and your faithfulness.
> Why should the nations say,
>     "Where is their God?"
>
> Our God is in the heavens!
>     He works everything that he desires.
> Their idols are silver and gold—
>     the work of human hands!
>
> They have mouths, but do not speak.
>     They have eyes, but do not see.
> They have ears, but do not hear.
>     They have noses, but do not smell.
> They have hands, but do not feel.
>     They have feet, but do not walk.
> They make no sound from their throats.
> Those who fashion them are just like them,
>     So are all who trust in them!
>
> O Israel, trust in the LORD!
>     He is their help and their shield.
> O house of Aaron, trust in the LORD!
>     He is their help and their shield.
> O you who fear the LORD, trust in the LORD!
>     He is their help and their shield. (vv. 1–11 AT)

Notice how the psalm is structured: An introduction (vv. 1–2) closes with a question: "Why should the nations say, 'Where is their God?'" The body of the psalm then unfolds in two halves. In the first half of the body (vv. 3–8), the psalmist literally answers the question, "Where is their God?" by asserting, "Our God is in the heavens!" (v. 3a). The psalmist then goes on to compare Israel's heaven-dwelling God with the idols that the nations worship. Israel's God "*works* everything that he desires." But the nations' idols are themselves the *works* of human hands—they are mute, blind, deaf, unable to smell or feel, and lame. And so are all those who trust in such idols.

In the second half of the psalm's body (vv. 9–18; only vv. 9–11 are quoted here for reasons of space), the psalmist shifts tones and now exhorts his audience. The psalm writer addresses "Israel" (the members of God's people gathered for worship), the "house of Aaron" (the company of priests gathered for worship), and those "who fear the LORD" (probably meaning non-Israelites who worship the Lord but have not formally been received into the people). The psalmist exhorts this audience to "trust in the LORD" (rather than trusting in the idols of the nations). So an abbreviated outline of the psalm's structure might look like this:

> **Question** (vv. 1–2)  Why should the nations say, "Where is their God?"
>
> **Answer** (vv. 3–8)  Our God is alive in the heavens (not a dead idol).
>
> **Exhortation** (vv. 9–18)  Trust in the living LORD.

Note: Take care to notice the extra line spaces that occur, respectively, between verses 2 and 3, and between 8 and 9. These spaces do not exist in the ancient Hebrew manuscripts from which our modern English Bibles are translated. Modern editors have added these spaces to make it easier for English readers to follow the structure of the psalms. As such, these spaces are *interpretations* of how the psalm is structured and where major and minor breaks in the psalm occur.

Psalms 15 and 24 also are examples of psalms that are marked with the question-answer structure. Psalm 15:1 asks, "O LORD, who may abide in your tent? Who may dwell on your holy hill?" (By this point you should notice and understand the parallelism of this question.) The rest of the psalm goes on to describe the qualifications of one who may enter God's presence. Similarly, Psalm 24:3 asks, "Who shall ascend the hill of the LORD? And who shall stand in his holy place?"

### Second Example: Division into Stanzas

A second common type of structure in the psalms consists of the division of a psalm into several equal (or mostly equal) stanzas. A very clear example of this is Psalm 114:

> [A]  When Israel went out from Egypt,
>       the house of Jacob from a people of strange language,
>    Judah became God's sanctuary,
>       Israel his dominion.

[B]   The sea looked and fled;
          Jordan turned back.
      The mountains skipped like rams,
          the hills like lambs.

[B′]  Why is it, O sea, that you flee?
          O Jordan, that you turn back?
      O mountains, that you skip like rams?
          O hills, like lambs?

[A′]  Tremble, O earth, at the presence of the LORD,
          at the presence of the God of Jacob,
      who turns the rock into a pool of water,
          the flint into a spring of water.

Psalm 114 is a clear example of how a psalm can be structured to have several equal stanzas. Each stanza consists of four lines of poetry. As we noted above with respect to Psalm 115, the extra line spaces that occur between each of the four stanzas are not present in the ancient Hebrew manuscripts from which the modern English versions are translated. Such spaces are the interpretations of expert translators, who make judgments about how to divide the psalm so that modern readers can understand the psalm more easily. But in the case of Psalm 114, the division is very clear. The stanzas that we have marked B and B′ are obviously similar. In both stanzas, each line shares identical words or phrases: "sea" and "fled"/"flee," "Jordan" and "turned back"/"turn back," "mountains" and "skipped"/"skip like rams," and "hills" "like lambs." And note also that stanzas A and A′ each mention "Jacob."

A second example of a psalm that is structured with equal stanzas is Psalm 46:

    [1] God is our refuge and strength,
          a very present help in trouble.
    [2] Therefore we will not fear, though the earth should change,
          though the mountains shake in the heart of the sea;
    [3] though its waters roar and foam,
          though the mountains tremble with its tumult.     *Selah*

    [4] There is a river whose streams make glad the city of God,
          the holy habitation of the Most High.
    [5] God is in the midst of the city; it shall not be moved;
          God will help it when the morning dawns.
    [6] The nations are in an uproar, the kingdoms totter;
          he utters his voice, the earth melts.

⁷ *The* LORD *of hosts is with us;*
     *the God of Jacob is our refuge.*            *Selah*

⁸ Come, behold the works of the LORD;
     see what desolations he has brought on the earth.
⁹ He makes wars cease to the end of the earth;
     he breaks the bow, and shatters the spear;
     he burns the shields with fire.
¹⁰ "Be still, and know that I am God!
     I am exalted among the nations,
     I am exalted in the earth."
¹¹ *The* LORD *of hosts is with us;*
     *the God of Jacob is our refuge.*            *Selah*

This psalm has three stanzas, each of which is three verses long. At the end of the second and third stanzas is a refrain (in italics here for emphasis): "The LORD of hosts is with us; the God of Jacob is our refuge." At the end of each stanza, the Hebrew word *Selah* also occurs. The meaning of this Hebrew word is no longer known. The best guess is that the word indicated some kind of musical instruction regarding the performance of the psalm in worship. But for our purposes, notice that the word functions to divide the psalm into three crisp stanzas. Some scholars have suggested that the refrain—"The LORD of hosts is with us; the God of Jacob is our refuge"—may originally have been included after verse 3. In other words, perhaps the psalm originally had three equal stanzas, each of which was followed by the refrain and then the word *Selah*.

How does understanding the structure of the psalm help a reader understand the meaning of the poem? In this case, understanding the structure of the psalm helps the reader grasp what it means to believe that "the LORD of hosts is with us, the God of Jacob is our stronghold" (AT). The first stanza of the psalm describes what some scholars call "natural evil": dangers and threats that come from the natural order, such as earthquakes, tsunamis, and the like. The second stanza focuses on what scholars refer to as "moral evil": dangers and threats that stem from human beings, such as war and oppression: "the nations are in an uproar, the kingdoms totter." The third stanza ends with God's speaking words that silence both the moral evil ("I am exalted among the nations") as well as the natural evil ("I am exalted in the earth"). Then the psalm closes with the refrain. In other words, stanzas 1 and 2 name two ways in which creation is in rebellion against God. Stanza 3 then describes God's response. And the refrain in turn gives the community words that express its faith.

Other psalms that are structured as stanzas include Psalms 2; 42–43; 107; and 139. These psalms are discussed elsewhere in this book.

### Third Example: Turning Points in Psalms

Some psalms have key turning points in which the mood or concept of the psalm makes a significant turn. The language of "turning point" was developed by the prominent psalms scholar Patrick Miller.[5] The term is helpful because it names the way in which some psalms are structured. It is often good for the reader of a psalm to look for the key point around which the meaning of the psalm pivots.

Psalm 73 is a good example of such a psalm. The psalm begins with a basic assertion: "Truly God is good to the upright" (v. 1a). But then the psalm describes how hard this faith statement is to accept because so often in life it seems as if the wicked prosper and the upright suffer (vv. 2–16). This section of the psalm can be summed up by two verses. The first is verse 3: "I was envious of the arrogant; I saw the prosperity of the wicked." The second is verse 16: "When I thought how to understand this, it seemed to me a wearisome task." The psalmist even admits that he was tempted to give up on God and join with the wicked. Then with verse 17 comes the turning point of the psalm: "until I went into the sanctuary of God; then I perceived their end." The great Old Testament theologian Walter Brueggemann says Psalm 73 "pivots on verse 17."[6] Brueggemann also calls the verse "the center of the psalm." He explains: "We would like to know more, but we are given only a hint. . . . In some ways—perhaps liturgical—the reality of God's holiness caused the speaker to reperceive the tempting alternative [to live like the wicked]." Brueggemann says that the psalmist experienced "a moment of utter inversion."[7] This moment was a turning point for the psalmist—and is the turning point of the psalm.

Another example of a psalm that is structured around a central turning point is Psalm 12, which begins with a vulnerable cry for help: "Help, O LORD, for there is no longer anyone who is godly; the faithful have disappeared from humankind" (v. 1). But the psalm ends with a note of quiet confidence: "You, O LORD, will protect us; you will guard us from this generation forever" (v. 7). How did the psalm writer travel from such a feeling of vulnerability to such security? The turning point comes in verse 5, where a promise from the Lord is spoken: "'I will now rise up,' says the LORD; 'I will place them in the

5. Patrick Miller, "*Yāpîaḥ* in Psalm XII 6 [= 12:5 NRSV]," *Vetus Testamentum* 29 (1979): 495–501. See also Miller, *They Cried to the Lord: The Form and Theology of Biblical Prayer* (Minneapolis: Fortress, 1994).

6. Walter Brueggemann, "Bounded by Obedience and Praise: The Psalms as Canon," in *The Psalms and the Life of Faith*, ed. Patrick Miller (Minneapolis: Fortress, 1995), 209.

7. Walter Brueggemann, *The Message of the Psalms: A Theological Commentary* (Minneapolis: Augsburg, 1984), 118.

## A RESTRUCTURING OF PSALM 23 IN *PALE RIDER*

Toward the beginning of the Western film *Pale Rider* (1985), a group of pros-
pectors and the village in which their families live have been attacked by the
villain, who is after their claims. To get them to give up their claims so that he
can begin strip-mining the land, the villain sends his strongmen to drive them
off. A daughter of the settlement, Megan (played by Sydney Penny), kneels
over the grave of her dog, killed in the attack, which she has just buried. She
then begins to recite an altered form of Psalm 23, and as she does, she re-
structures the psalm, turning it into a dialogue of the psalmist's voice and her
own interjections:

> The LORD is my shepherd,
>   I shall not want.
>     —*But I do want.*—
> . . . He leadeth me beside still waters;
> he restoreth my soul.
>     —*But they killed my dog.*—
> Yea though I walk through the valley
>   of the shadow of death,
> I shall fear no evil;
>     —*But I am afraid.*—
>   for thou art with me;
> thy rod and thy staff—they comfort me.
>     —*But we need a miracle.*—
> Thy loving-kindness and mercy
>   shall follow me all the days of my life,
>     —*If you exist.*—
> and I shall dwell
>   in the house of the LORD forever.
>     —*But I'd like to get more of this life first.*

safety for which they long.'" So the structure of the psalm might be described
something like this: a human cry for help, followed by a promising response
from the Lord, followed by a human expression of trust.

### Anatomy of a Psalm

When authors write about the psalms, they use special terms to refer to various
parts of the psalms. The figure "Anatomy of a Psalm" (see p. 28) illustrates
the meaning of these terms.

# Anatomy of a Psalm

## Psalm 89 "God's Covenant with David"

¹ *A Maskil of Ethan the Ezrahite.*

I will sing of your steadfast love, O Lᴏʀᴅ, forever;
    with my mouth I will proclaim your faithfulness to all generations.
² I declare that your steadfast love is established forever;
    your faithfulness is as firm as the heavens.
³ You said, "I have made a covenant with my chosen one,
    I have sworn to my servant David:
⁴ 'I will establish your descendants forever,
    and build your throne for all generations.'" *Selah*

Verses 5–51

⁵ Let the heavens praise your wonders, O Lᴏʀᴅ,
    your faithfulness in the assembly of the holy ones.

. . . . . . . . . . . . . . . . . . . . . . . . . . . . . . . . . . . . .

⁵⁰ Remember, O Lᴏʀᴅ, how your servant is taunted;
    how I bear in my bosom the insults of the peoples,
⁵¹ with which your enemies taunt, O Lᴏʀᴅ,
    with which they taunted the footsteps of your anointed.
⁵² Blessed be the Lᴏʀᴅ forever. Amen and Amen.

## Conclusion

In this chapter, the reader was introduced to the basic features of Hebrew poetry, based on the assumption that in order to read the psalms with understanding, a reader needs to grasp the basic governing logic of how Hebrew poetry creates meaning. First, the reader was introduced to Hebrew parallelism. It was argued that parallelism operates on multiple levels: between words (parallelism that works within a phrase), between phrases (parallelism that works within a verse), between verses (parallelism that works within a stanza), between stanzas (parallelism that works within a psalm), and between psalms (parallelism that works to create "twin psalms" or pairs of psalms). The reader was also introduced to the idea of poetic structure of psalms and to poetic development within a psalm.

---

### GOING DEEPER

In order to deepen your understanding of the concepts in this chapter, consider doing one or more of the following exercises:

1. Find someone who has not studied Hebrew poetry and try to explain the concept of Hebrew parallelism in a way that they can understand it.
2. Open up a Bible to the book of Psalms and pick any psalm. See if you can track both the way that parallelism is working in the psalm and the way that the psalm develops poetically.
3. Think about a question that you have asked or that someone has asked you in the last week. Write a six-line psalm about the question. Construct the psalm so that the first two lines ask the question by using Hebrew parallelism, and the last four lines answer the question by again using Hebrew parallelism.

---

### FOR FURTHER READING

Alter, Robert. *The Art of Biblical Poetry*. Rev. ed. New York: Basic Books, 2011.

Berlin, Adele. *The Dynamics of Biblical Parallelism*. Bloomington: Indiana University Press, 1985.

———. "Introduction to Hebrew Poetry." In *The New Interpreter's Bible: A Commentary in Twelve Volumes*, 4:301–15. Nashville: Abingdon, 1996.

Fokkelman, J. P. *Reading Biblical Poetry: An Introductory Guide.* Louisville: Westminster John Knox, 2001.

Gillingham, Susan E. *The Poems and Psalms of the Hebrew Bible.* Oxford: Oxford University Press, 1994.

Kugel, James. *The Idea of Biblical Poetry.* New Haven: Yale University Press, 1981.

# TWO

# What Is a Psalm?

### *Learning to Understand Different Psalm Genres—Part 1*

Consider the meaning of the following phrase:

Clean Bathrooms!!!

The meaning is obvious, right? Not so fast, my friend. Depending on *the context* in which these words occur, they can mean radically different things.

On the one hand, imagine that you find these words on a note taped to your door, which has been written and placed there by someone you live with—such as a parent, a spouse, or a roommate. Imagine that the note also includes these other words: "Take out the garbage!" and "Do the dishes!" and "Put away your laundry!" and finally, "The guests arrive at 6:30!!" In such a context, the meaning of the words will be clear to you—they are *a commandment*. You will know that you are expected to clean the bathrooms—preferably before your parent, spouse, or roommate returns. Furthermore, the three exclamation points after the words "clean bathrooms" and the last line about the guests arriving at 6:30 might indicate an order of priority and purpose to the list. Because your housemate does not want to be embarrassed, you had better start with those tasks that will be most visible—cleaning the bathrooms, taking out the garbage, getting the kitchen in order. If you don't, there might be a scene later.

On the other hand, imagine that the above words are found in a different context. You pull your car off the highway and ease it into a gas station. On a professionally printed sign suspended over the entrance to the gas station, you read these words: "Clean Bathrooms!!!" On the same sign you read "Fresh Baked Goods!" and "Free Coffee Made Hourly!" and "Under New Management!" In such a context, the meaning of the words will be clear to you: they are *a promise*. Within this context, you would know that these words imply an expectation of what you can find inside the gas station: welcoming management, a clean restroom, fresh coffee and food. In short, you can expect to feel comfortable.

Notice three things about these examples. First, the above illustration is describing two different literary contexts. The technical term for this is two different genres. In the first example, the words "Clean Bathrooms!!!" are encountered in the context of a *to-do list*. In the second example, the words are encountered in the context of an *advertisement*. Second, in two different literary contexts, identical words can mean totally different things. In the first example, the words indicate a command *for the reader to do something*. In the second example, the words indicate a promise *that something has been done for the reader*. Third, in order to understand the written words correctly, a reader must be able to identify the correct genre in which the words occur. *A competent reader is equipped with the skill to identify the literary genre in which words occur, which helps the reader experience the words correctly.*

This chapter is about equipping the reader to understand the different genres of the psalms so that the reader can experience the psalms authentically and understand them more completely. In the introduction, we cited John Ciardi's maxim, "Analysis is never in any sense a substitute for the poem. The best any analysis can do is to prepare the reader to enter the poem more perceptively."[1] In this chapter the reader will be introduced to some of the different genres of the psalms so that the reader may enter those poems more perceptively. But remember, the purpose of the analysis is not the analysis for its own sake; it is to equip the reader to enter the psalm.

Reading the psalms requires using this skill over and over—identifying which genre of psalm one is reading and then using that identification to help in understanding the words that one reads. *The competent reader of the psalms is able to identify what genre a particular psalm is, which thus enables the reader to understand the meaning of the words that occur in that psalm.*

---

1. John Ciardi, *How Does a Poem Mean?* (New York: Houghton Mifflin, 1959), 663.

## Introducing the Concept of Genre in the Psalms

There are 150 psalms in the book of Psalms. That invites a simple question: "What is a psalm anyway?" Like many good questions, there is the short and simple answer, and then there is the long and complicated answer. First, the short, simple answer. A psalm is a biblical poem. The English word "psalm" is derived from the Greek *psalmos*, which in turn was used to translate the Hebrew word *mizmor*, which literally means "song." So in the most basic sense, a psalm is a biblical song or poem.

Second, the longer and more complicated answer. There are many different types of psalms. As an example, take the following song, which was sung by David at the death of his friend Jonathan:

David took up this lament concerning Saul and his son Jonathan, and he ordered that the people of Judah be taught this lament of the bow (it is written in the Book of Jashar):

"A gazelle lies slain on your heights, Israel.
  How the mighty have fallen!

"Tell it not in Gath,
    proclaim it not in the streets of Ashkelon,
lest the daughters of the Philistines be glad,
    lest the daughters of the uncircumcised rejoice.

"Mountains of Gilboa,
    may you have neither dew nor rain,
    may no showers fall on your terraced fields.
For there the shield of the mighty was despised,
    the shield of Saul—no longer rubbed with oil.

"From the blood of the slain,
    from the flesh of the mighty,
the bow of Jonathan did not turn back,
    the sword of Saul did not return unsatisfied.
Saul and Jonathan—
    in life they were loved and admired,
    and in death they were not parted.
They were swifter than eagles,
    they were stronger than lions.

"Daughters of Israel,
    weep for Saul,
who clothed you in scarlet and finery,
    who adorned your garments with ornaments of gold.

"How the mighty have fallen in battle!
    Jonathan lies slain on your heights.
I grieve for you, Jonathan my brother;
    you were very dear to me.
Your love for me was wonderful,
    more wonderful than that of women.

"How the mighty have fallen!
    The weapons of war have perished!" (2 Sam. 1:17–27 NIV)

David's song on the occasion of the deaths of Saul and Jonathan is an example of a psalm that occurs outside of the book of Psalms—in one of the narrative books of the Bible. The psalms in these books teach us things that we might not otherwise know about the psalms. This psalm shows us that psalms were sung not only in the temple during worship but also in the course of daily life—out in the fields, so to speak. This song is a certain type of psalm—a "lament" (v. 17); the Hebrew word for this is *qinah* (pronounced *qee-NAH*), a song one sings in mourning after the death of a loved one. The *qinah* songs have an identifiable, metered rhythm in Hebrew. They celebrated the life and deeds of the deceased as they also expressed grief over the loss.

The reason that the second answer to the question "What is a psalm?" is long and complicated is that there are many different *genres* of biblical poems; until you have explained all of the genres of the psalms, you have not yet fully answered the question of what a psalm is. In the rest of this chapter and in chapter 3, the reader will explore the many different subtypes or subcategories of biblical poems.

Outside of the Bible, there are also different subtypes of poems. In Japanese poetry, for example, a haiku is a particular genre of poetry.

A haiku is sparse and tightly controlled. Normally, a haiku has seventeen syllables in three lines (five, seven, and five syllables, respectively); it must compare two images and use a word for a season of the year. Or again, in English language poetry, a limerick is a subtype of poem. A limerick has a trotting, amphibrachic meter[2] and consists of five lines that have a strict AABBA rhyme scheme. Limericks are usually humorous (and quite often they are obscene). When a person experiences these two very different genres of poetry, the competent reader expects to have very different experiences. And, of course, there are many other genres of poems: sonnets (which have fourteen

---

2. Meaning that each segment of poetic meter has three syllables: a short one, next a long one, then a short one.

---

### CONTEXT SAVES LIVES

In the example of the words "Clean Bathrooms!!!" found on a to-do list, imagine that you ignore the implied commandment. The note's author returns home, finds dirty dishes in the sink and you watching television, and demands, "Did you get the list done? The guests will be here in forty-five minutes!" You reply, "I misunderstood. I thought you meant that you had already cleaned the bathrooms, taken out the trash, done the dishes, and all was ready for the guests to arrive." How do you think that conversation would go?

Try to think of a time when you misunderstood something that you had been told or something that you had read—a voicemail, a text, a question on a test, or an overheard part of one side of a phone conversation. Why did you misunderstand what you heard or read? What extra context would you have needed to have understood it more fully?

---

lines), ballads (which tell stories), quatrain poetry (in which each stanza has four lines and lines 2 and 4 must rhyme), and so on.

The term "genre" means a category, type, or form of literature. A "psalm" itself is a genre of literature. But within the broader genre we call psalms, there are subgenres (smaller categories) of psalms. There are lamentations, prayers for help, hymns, songs of thanksgiving, and songs of trust—to name just five. Each of these different types of psalms is a different "genre." In general, the concept of genre is a basic part of what makes literature work. In order for a written composition to be understandable, the author and audience must share some common assumptions about the genre of what the author is writing. The genre of a piece of literature will often determine how an interpreter will understand the meaning of words. Each genre comes with its own set of characteristic elements and assumptions. These include such things as the following:

1. The *situation* and the *speaker*: assumptions about who is speaking and assumptions about what has happened or is happening in the speaker's life;

2. The *audience*: what kind of audience is being addressed;

3. The *language*: what kinds of sentences (questions, requests, exclamations, declarations, etc.) and what meaning or content are appropriate (expressions of trust, cries of pain or doubt, joyous exclamations of emotion, etc.).

## Two Types of Genre: Content and Form

Consider the following items:

How would you separate the above items into two groups? On the one hand, as an interpreter (basically someone who is trying to understand something) you could focus mainly on the *external forms* of the items. In that case, you might group the first two items together in one category because both share a similar form, but the third item you could place in a separate category. On the other hand, if as an interpreter you focus mainly on the *internal content* of the items, you might group the second and third items together in a category because both share similar content, and you might assign the first item to a separate category. Notice that, as an interpreter, you were first asked to look for patterns of similarities and differences in the shapes, and then to assign categories to those patterns. When interpreting the psalms, readers do a similar thing.

Interpreters of the psalms seek to understand the psalms. Thus, in order to understand the psalms and "enter into them," interpreters have found it helpful to look for patterns of similarities and differences between psalms.

What interpreters have found when they have looked for similarities and differences in patterns between psalms is that some psalms share a similar *form*, and other psalms share similar *content*. In terms of form, some psalms begin and end the same, or share a similar structure, or seem to have quite similar types of sentences. But other psalms have similar content: they share common themes, such as mentioning the king (called royal psalms) or nature (creation psalms) or focusing on the city of Jerusalem (psalms of Zion) or asking for forgiveness (penitential psalms). Chapter 3 will introduce the reader to genres of psalms that share similar content.

In the rest of this chapter, the reader will be introduced to genres of psalms that share similar forms. There will be information about the forms of each genre, about what a competent reader assumes about the speaker, and so on. But remember, the purpose of this analysis is not just to learn that these various psalm genres exist. Rather, the purpose is to prepare the reader to enter the various types of poems in the Psalter "more perceptively" (in the words of Ciardi).

## "Help Me! Help Me! Help Me!"—Prayers for Help (Lament Psalms)

Consider the following biblical poem. Based only on the words of the poem, enter into the poem and wonder about three things: (1) What do you think has happened or is happening in the speaker's life that would call forth these words? (2) To whom is the speaker talking and why? (3) Why is the speaker choosing to use specific words or specific types of sentences?

> [1] How long, O LORD? Will you forget me forever?
>     How long will you hide your face from me?
> [2] How long must I bear pain in my soul,
>     and have sorrow in my heart all day long?
> How long shall my enemy be exalted over me?
>
> [3] Consider and answer me, O LORD my God!
>     Give light to my eyes, or I will sleep the sleep of death,
> [4] and my enemy will say, "I have prevailed";
>     my foes will rejoice because I am shaken.
>
> [5] But I trusted in your steadfast love;
>     my heart shall rejoice in your salvation.
> [6] I will sing to the LORD,
>     because he has dealt bountifully with me. (Ps. 13)

There are a range of possible answers to the above questions. What is happening in the speaker's life? Something terribly upsetting has apparently happened. The speaker has experienced a crisis of some sort and thus talks of "pain in my soul" and "sorrow in my heart." This psalmist also speaks of "my enemy" who oppresses—perhaps this refers to one or more actual people, but it might refer to something else. Clearly, the speaker is addressing God, asking questions ("How long, O LORD?"), calling for help ("answer me"), expressing trust ("I trusted in your steadfast love"), and making a promise ("I will sing . . .").

What kind of a poem is this?

This psalm (Ps. 13) is an example of the most common type of psalm in the Psalter: a prayer for help. Such psalms are also often referred to as *psalms of lament* because they cry out to God in complaint: they lament. We prefer to call them prayers for help because the center of gravity in these poems is not the complaint but rather the request: the psalmists ask for God's help, in the belief that God can help if God chooses to. Roughly one-third of the psalms are prayers for help.[3]

3. Different scholars categorize psalms differently, but psalms often considered to be prayers for help include Pss. 3; 4; 5; 7; 9–10; 13; 17; 22; 26; 28; 31; 35; 36; 38; 39; 42–43; 44; 51; 54; 55;

Psalm 13 is a good example of a prayer for help because it includes all of the major elements that may be typically found in these psalms: situation of crisis, address to God, complaint, request for help, expression of trust, and promise to praise.

### The Situation: Crisis!

Like all of the prayers for help, Psalm 13 seems to be spoken in the midst of some personal crisis. In some psalms, there are some hints about what the crisis might be: a severe illness, oppression by an enemy, an accusation that one has committed a crime, an impending military battle, or something similar. But in many psalms, as is the case with Psalm 13, the language used is vague, and one cannot identify any particular crisis. Likely the ambiguity about the psalmist's situation is intentional: these psalms refer to crisis in only vague terms so that many people in the midst of many different crises will be able to pray these psalms.

Read Psalm 13 again. As you do, ask two questions: (1) Were there circumstances in my own life when the words of Psalm 13 might have "fit"? If so, what were those times? (2) Do I know anyone right now whose situation might fit these words?

### The Primary Audience: God

Psalm 13, like all prayers for help, is spoken to God. The psalm addresses God by using the words "O Lord" and "my God" and simply "you." In other psalms, various phrases are used, such as "God of my right!" (4:1), "my King" (5:2), "my shield" (7:10), "God of our salvation" (79:9), "my rock" (62:2), and "my refuge" (61:3). The point of this address to God is that these poems are prayers. God is the primary audience for these poems. The psalmist assumes an ongoing relationship with God (notice that God is *my* God, *my* king, *my* shield, God of *our* salvation). But observe also that the images used for God are images of protection, safety, and power: rock, shield, refuge, king, and the like. By using those words for God, those speaking the psalms were subtly calling on God for protection, safety, and powerful deliverance.

The images that the psalms use to address God were taken from the daily life of the ancient world. Are there comparable images or concepts in today's daily life that might evoke protection, safety, and powerful deliverance?

---

56; 57; 58; 59; 60; 61; 67; 69; 70; 71; 74; 77; 79; 80; 82; 83; 85; 86; 88; 89; 90; 94; 102; 108; 109; 120; 123; 126; 130; 137; 139; 140; 141; 142; 143; 144.

### The Secondary Audience: The Human Community

In the main, these "prayers for help" are addressed to God. In Psalm 13, the entire poem is spoken directly to Israel's God, who is known as "the LORD." But consider the following verses, which are also from prayers for help:

> How long will you people turn my glory into shame?
> How long will you love delusions and seek false gods? (4:2 NIV)

> Sing the praises of the LORD, enthroned in Zion;
> proclaim among the nations what he has done. (9:11 NIV)

> Love the LORD, all you his saints!
> The LORD preserves the faithful, (31:23b NRSV)
> but the proud he pays back in full! (31:23c NIV)

> Cast your cares on the LORD,
> and he will sustain you;
> He will never let the righteous be shaken! (55:22 NIV)

These four examples all come from prayers for help. The sentences are addressed not directly to God but to other human beings. Although such sentences are rare in prayers for help, they nevertheless suggest that these prayers have a secondary audience: the human community. The pray-ers of these poems seem to be aware that their prayers are being overheard. And the pray-ers of the psalms would like for their community to accept them and to learn from their plight.

What might this poetic awareness of a secondary audience mean for modern readers of these poems? First, modern readers can think of themselves as the secondary audience when they overhear the prayers of the psalmists. What might it mean to overhear the prayer of another person? In these prayers, the psalmists cry out in pain and name their needs. When a person overhears the cries of pain and expressed needs of one who is suffering, does that person have a moral obligation to the person they are overhearing—either to help ease their pain or meet their needs? If so, what does it mean to listen in on the prayer of a long-dead sufferer?

### The Language (Part 1): Complaint (Lament)

How would you describe the following language?

> How long, O LORD? Will you forget me forever?
> How long will you hide your face from me?

> How long must I bear pain in my soul,
>     and have sorrow in my heart all day long?
> How long shall my enemy be exalted over me? (13:1–2)

Those who analyze the psalms have described this speech as "complaint" or "lament." All prayers for help include complaints about the psalmist's situation of crisis. These complaints can come in any (or all) of three forms—the "you complaint," the "I complaint," and the "they complaint." In the "you complaint," the psalmist complains to God *about* God. In Psalm 13, the "you complaint" is in verse 1: "How long, O LORD? Will you forget me forever?" In the "I complaint," the psalmist complains about one's own suffering. In Psalm 13, we read, "How long must I bear pain in my soul?" In the "they complaint," the psalmist complains about other human beings who are contributing to the psalmist's suffering. Some of these other humans seem to have been enemies who oppressed the psalmist; others may have been community members who simply did not support or help the psalmist. In Psalm 13, the psalmist complains, "How long shall my enemy be exalted over me?" It is often characteristic of the complaint parts of a psalm that they ask questions of God ("How long?" or "Why do you hide yourself?" [10:1] or "Where is your steadfast love?" [89:49]). In prayers for help, questioning God—even accusing God—was not seen as being unfaithful or lacking in trust. It was considered a vital and even necessary part of the faith relationship.

Central to these psalms, expressed in the complaint sections, is a simple assertion: life should not be this way. The psalmists cry out in pain, expressing the fundamental belief that the world need not be as it is, that life should not be as painful and dangerous as it sometimes is.

### The Language (Part 2): Request for Help

Next, consider the following verses from Psalm 13. How would you describe them?

> Consider and answer me, O LORD my God!
>     Give light to my eyes, or I will sleep the sleep of death,
> and my enemy will say, "I have prevailed";
>     my foes will rejoice because I am shaken. (vv. 3–4)

The most important part of each prayer for help is the request for help. In Psalm 13, the pray-er asks, "Give light to my eyes, or I will sleep the sleep of death." In other psalms, the psalmist prays such petitions as "Deliver me" (3:7), "Answer me" (4:1), "Lead me" (5:8), "Save my life" (6:4), "Rise up" (7:6), and many similar cries. In most prayers for help, the psalmist asks more than one thing. In Psalm 17, for example, the psalmist pleads, "Hear a just cause," "Attend to my cry," "Show your steadfast love," "Guard me," "Hide me," "Rise up," "Confront them"—and that is not an exhaustive list! In each of these psalms, the psalmist does not think of these prayers as personal meditations but as part of an active, ongoing relationship with one who is greater and more powerful than the psalmist or those who are oppressing the psalmist.

As part of the request for help, these psalms also often include phrases that urge God or offer motivating reasons for God to answer the prayer. Here, the psalmist says, "or I will sleep the sleep of death" (13:3). This phrase, as is the case with other psalms, asserts that the extreme nature of the psalmist's crisis is a reason for God to answer the prayer. In other psalms, the pray-ers cite God's nature as reason for answering: God is urged to act "according to your steadfast love" or "for your goodness' sake" (25:7). Still other psalms cite either the innocence of the psalmist ("If you test me, you will find no wickedness in me" [17:3])[4] or the guilt of those enemies who oppress ("They close their hearts to pity; with their mouths they speak arrogantly" [17:10]). Patrick Miller has written that these motivating and urging phrases

> appeal to God to be and to act as God would be and act. Here prayer is not simply "Thy will be done." . . . The motive clauses are, in effect, a way of indicating that God's response to the cry for help should be a manifestation of mercy and love, a demonstration of God's just dealing in the world, a compassionate response to the sufferer in pain or to the weak and powerless in the community, an act of righteousness in that God's help will be appropriate to the relationship established between God and the people.[5]

### The Language (Part 3): Expression of Trust

How would you describe this language:

> But I trusted in your steadfast love;
> my heart shall rejoice in your salvation. (13:5)

Most of the prayers for help also include sections in which the psalmist expresses trust. In Psalm 13, the psalmist confesses, "But I trusted in your steadfast love." In other psalms, examples of statements of trust include these:

---

4. Here the psalmist is not claiming never to have done anything wrong, only that in whatever crisis there is *right now*, in this particular matter the poet has done nothing wrong.

5. Patrick Miller, *They Cried to the Lord: The Form and Theology of Biblical Prayer* (Minneapolis: Fortress, 1994), 126.

"As for me, I shall behold your face in righteousness" (17:15). "Yet you are holy, enthroned on the praises of Israel. In you our ancestors trusted, and you delivered them" (22:3–4). "O my God, in you I trust" (25:2). "This I know, that God is for me" (56:9). And so on. The appearance of these calm expressions of trust right next to the agitated complaints that we saw earlier can confuse interpreters—especially modern interpreters who long for consistency. At this point, suffice it to say that just as the questions and accusations in these psalms were not seen as a lack of faith on the part of the pray-ers, so also these expressions of trust do not mean that the crisis had passed for the psalmists. Such expressions of trust do not signal simply a shift in mood. Rather, they signal that in the midst of the crisis, the psalmist's faith included hoping in and clinging to the faithfulness of God—often in the absence of any external reason for such hope.

### The Language (Part 4): Promise to Praise

Finally, consider the following verse:

> I will sing to the Lord,
>     because he has dealt bountifully with me. (13:6)

Prayers for help also often include promises to praise God once the time of crisis has passed. In Psalm 13, the closing verses are such a promise: "My heart shall rejoice in your salvation. I will sing to the Lord." Similar promises to praise can be found in many other psalms, for example: "I will give to the Lord thanks due to his righteousness" (7:17). "In the great congregation I will bless the Lord" (26:12). To understand these promises to praise, one needs to understand that praise was understood first and foremost as testimony about what God had done (more on this below). The psalmist promises to let others know what God has done after receiving God's help. These promises are not bargaining with God, as they are sometimes misinterpreted; rather, they are an extension of the expression of trust. They indicate the psalmist's enduring commitment to God.

The prayers for help are generally divided into two broad types: the prayer for help of the individual (such as Ps. 13) and the prayer for help of the community (such as Pss. 44 and 82). The prayers for help of the individuals are far more numerous in the Psalter than the prayers for help of the community. As these labels make clear, prayer for help was both a matter for individuals amid some difficulty and a matter for the community when facing a major crisis.

## "God Is Good; You Should Get to Know Him"—Hymns of Praise

The hymn of praise is the second most common type of psalm in the Psalter.[6] As the title of the genre indicates, the hymn was a song primarily intended to be sung in communal worship. And as indicated in the previous section, *the main purpose of praise is to tell who God is by telling what God has done.* Praise therefore is *testimony* or *witness*: it is a form of song in which the gathered community bears witness in song to who God is.

Psalm 113 is a typical hymn of praise:

> [1] Praise the LORD!
> Praise, O servants of the LORD;
> > praise the name of the LORD.
>
> [2] Blessed be the name of the LORD
> > from this time on and forevermore.
> [3] From the rising of the sun to its setting
> > the name of the LORD is to be praised.
> [4] The LORD is high above all nations,
> > and his glory above the heavens.
>
> [5] Who is like the LORD our God,
> > who is seated on high,
> [6] who looks far down
> > on the heavens and the earth?
> [7] He raises the poor from the dust,
> > and lifts the needy from the ash heap,
> [8] to make them sit with princes,
> > with the princes of his people.
> [9] He gives the barren woman a home,
> > making her the joyous mother of children.
> Praise the LORD!

Psalm 113 is a good model of the hymn of praise because it clearly shows the two main features of the hymn: (1) A call to praise and (2) unfolding testimony about who God is and what God has done.[7]

---

6. The hymns of praise may be identified as Pss. 8; 33; 47; 48; 65; 66; 67; 68; 76; 84; 87; 89; 93; 96; 97; 98; 99; 100; 103; 104; 105; 111; 112; 113; 114; 117; 135; 136; 145; 146; 147; 148; 149; 150.

7. In many, if not most, introductions of the psalms, the section of the hymns that we here call "testimony about what God has done" is referred to as "reasons for praise." See, for example, Claus Westermann, *The Psalms: Structure, Content, and Message* (Minneapolis: Augsburg, 1980), 90; and Miller, *They Cried to the Lord*, 206. But note also Miller's comment that after the call to praise, "the hymn continues with the expression of praise itself in a causal clause, usually beginning with *ki*, 'for,' that gives *a reason for praise* in some characteristic or activity of God."

### The Language (Part 1): Call to Praise

Most hymns begin and end with a call to praise. The most characteristic form of the call to praise is the one that is found at the beginning of Psalm 113: the Hebrew phrase *halelu-yah*, which literally means "Praise Yah(weh)!" (and thus is translated, "Praise the LORD!"). Other calls to praise include "Rejoice in the LORD!" (33:1), "Clap your hands!" (47:1), "Make a joyful noise to God!" (66:1), "Sing to the LORD!" (98:1), and "Bless the LORD!" (103:1). The point of the call to praise is to invite a community of worshipers into a celebratory expression of faith. The call to praise is itself an act of praise; for example, in some psalms such as Psalm 150, the entire psalm is nothing but a series of calls to praise. To invite the community to celebrate God's goodness is already to begin to celebrate. The call to praise sets the mood for praise: it is joyful, unrestrained, glad, celebratory. The call to praise also shows the goal of praise: to form a community of disciples. Praise is not just about God; it is also about the human community that belongs to God. These two actions—*to begin to celebrate* and *to form a community of disciples*—are what the call to praise is all about.

### The Situation and Primary Audience of the Hymn of Praise

Notice, already, two things that are radically different about the hymn of praise when compared to the prayer for help. On the one hand, the prayer for help assumes a time of crisis, and the primary audience to which the prayer is addressed is God. The hymn of praise, on the other hand, has *the human community* as its primary audience. And although the hymn can be sung in good times as well as bad, we can at least say that the hymn does not assume a time of crisis.

Many of the hymns close by reiterating the call to praise. This is an artful way to end a song—bringing the movement of the song "full circle," as it were. But it also signals that praise is not a one-and-done sort of affair. Rather, praise is ongoing: praise is a way of life.

### The Language (Part 2): Testimony about Who God Is and What God Has Done

The second major feature of the hymn of praise is often the body or heart of these psalms. These sections of the hymns often (but not always) start out with the word "for." For example, in Psalm 117, the shortest of all the psalms, the singer says,

> [1] Praise the LORD, all you nations!
>     Extol him, all you peoples!

² For great is his steadfast love toward us,
>     and the faithfulness of the LORD endures forever!
Praise the LORD!

In this second part of these psalms, the singer expands from the call to praise forward into the expression of praise itself. Claus Westermann has offered a compelling metaphor that helps the reader understand the relationship between the initial call to praise and the unfolding testimony that makes up the body of these psalms:

> [The structure of the hymn of praise] might be viewed from the situation of a hiker who has discovered, as he was walking a bit apart from the path his group had taken, a marvelous view of the landscape. He calls the others to come and view it, and their joint viewing becomes an awestruck, marveling description of the view before them.[8]

The call to praise—like the beckoning of the hiker who has discovered the view—is the invitation to come and take in the marvelous view. The unfolding testimony about who God is and what God has done is the experience itself, the experience of joining in and drinking up the vast, panoramic view.

As already noted, the main body of these hymns of praise describes who God is by telling what God has done. In Psalm 113 the poem does this by using paradoxical imagery to describe the Lord as the God whose being is unreachably transcendent: "The LORD is high above all nations, and his glory above the heavens" (v. 4). Yet God's way of being in the world is to act in the lowest, most earthy places: "Who looks far down . . . [and] raises the poor from the dust, and lifts the needy from the ash heap" (vv. 6a, 7). The other hymns of praise tell who God is by describing a vast array of God's gracious actions. A few examples here will be enough to whet the reader's appetite to do more exploration. The Lord "provides food for those who fear him" (111:5a), "has established the world" (93:1c), "is faithful in all his words, and gracious in all his deeds" (145:13b), "sets the prisoners free, . . . opens the eyes of the blind, . . . lifts up those who are bowed down" (146:7c–8b), "forgives all your iniquity, . . . heals all your diseases" (103:3), and so on.

Within *unfolding-testimony* sections of the hymns, different types of language are used. In the first form, the singers speak *about* God by using third-person nouns and pronouns. In the second form, the singers speak *to* God by using second-person nouns and pronouns. In the first type of praise, which describes God's character and actions in the third person, *the goal is to give*

---

8. Westermann, *The Psalms*, 85.

*God away to the neighbor*. For example, in Psalm 117, which was quoted above, the unfolding-testimony section of the psalm speaks of God in the third person: "For great is his steadfast love toward us, and the faithfulness of the LORD endures forever!" In this form of praise, the singer or singers bear witness to others—telling others who God is by telling what God has done. In the words of Patrick Miller, this type of praise is *"testimony for conversion."*[9] Such praise seeks "to bear witness to all who hear that God is God."[10]

There is also a second way in which the hymns respond to the call to praise in unfolding testimony and praise. In this second form, the singers speak directly to God in the second person. For example, consider this section of Psalm 92:

> For you, O LORD, have made me glad by your work;
>     at the works of your hands I sing for you. (v. 4)

If the goal of the first form of praise is for the psalmist to give God away to the neighbor, in the second form of praise *the goal is for the singer to give oneself away to God*. In the first form of praise, the goal is witness: the psalmist wants the neighbor to share in the joy of a relationship with God. In this second form of praise, the goal is piety: the psalmist yearns to draw closer to God. As J. Clinton McCann has written, the goal in this form of praise is "the offering of the whole self to God."[11] In this sort of praise, the finite and mortal human being longs to join one's being to something infinitely greater than oneself. To praise God directly as "you" is to join in proper conversation with God, in the manner in which a disciple joins in conversation with a master, or a young child joins in conversation with a parent. It acknowledges that the relationship is not one of equals—and that this is a good thing, for the Lord provides the singers with things that they cannot provide for themselves. In short, when the psalmists praise God directly by using second-person nouns and pronouns, they are giving themselves away fully to God.

## "I Am Holding On as Tightly as I Can, God"—Trust Psalms

A third basic genre of psalm is the psalm of trust. The psalm of trust is similar to the prayer for help in several ways and different in at least one key

---

9. Patrick Miller, *Interpreting the Psalms* (Philadelphia: Fortress, 1986), 68 (emphasis original).

10. Miller, *Interpreting the Psalms*, 68.

11. J. Clinton McCann, *A Theological Introduction to the Book of Psalms* (Nashville: Abingdon, 1993), 53.

aspect. Like the prayer for help, the psalm of trust can be spoken by either a community or an individual. For example, Psalm 46 is a communal psalm of trust that confesses, "The LORD of Hosts is with us; the God of Jacob is our refuge" (vv. 7, 11). However, Psalm 23 is an individual psalm of trust that confesses, "You are with me, your rod and your staff—they comfort me" (v. 4).

### The Situation: Crisis

Also similar to the prayer for help, the psalm of trust seems to assume a situation of crisis. For example, Psalms 22 and 69, both prayers for help, speak of being in the midst of deep distress: "I am poured out like water, and all my bones are out of joint. . . . For dogs are all around me; a company of evildoers encircles me" (22:14, 16). "The waters have come up to my neck. I sink in deep mire, where there is no foothold; I have come into deep water, and the flood sweeps over me" (69:1–2). Notice how the psalms of trust use very similar language as the prayers for help to describe the crises in which they find themselves. Psalm 46, which as already mentioned is a communal psalm of trust, describes a crisis in which "the mountains shake in the heart of the sea" and "the nations are in an uproar, the kingdoms totter" (vv. 2, 6). Similarly, the individual songs of trust in Psalms 23 and 27 describe walking "through the valley of the shadow of death" (23:4 KJV) and how "evildoers assail me to devour my flesh" (27:2). The two different genres of psalms express trust in God. The singer of the prayer for help in Psalm 13, as already noted, says, "But I trusted in your steadfast love" (v. 5). Similarly, in Psalm 23, the singer says, "I fear no evil; for you are with me" (v. 4).

As the name "psalm of trust" indicates, the primary difference between this type of psalm and the prayer for help is that in the psalm of trust, *the dominant mood or emotion is trust*. In the prayers for help, the expressions of trust are subordinate to the requests for help. In the psalms of trust, however, the requests for help are almost entirely lacking, with the result that the expressions of trust completely dominate.

The most well known of all the psalms is a psalm of trust—Psalm 23.[12]

> [1] The LORD is my shepherd, I shall not want.
>> [2] He makes me lie down in green pastures;
> he leads me beside still waters;
>> [3] he restores my soul.
> He leads me in right paths
>> for his name's sake.

12. Other psalms of trust include 11; 16; 27; 46; 52; 62; 63; 121; 125; 129; 131. Certain other psalms, such as 61 and 91, are also often described as psalms of trust.

⁴Even though I walk through the darkest valley,
  I fear no evil;
for you are with me;
  your rod and your staff—they comfort me.

⁵You prepare a table before me
  in the presence of my enemies;
you anoint my head with oil;
  my cup overflows.
⁶Surely goodness and mercy shall follow me
  all the days of my life,
and I shall dwell in the house of the LORD
  my whole life long.

As with other psalms of trust, this psalm exhibits the three general characteristic elements of the form: descriptions of threat, expressions of trust, and descriptions of God's care.

### The Language (Part 1): Descriptions of Threat

The psalms of trust generally describe, either metaphorically or literally, a genuine threat or danger. As noted above, Psalm 46 describes how "the mountains shake in the heart of the sea" and "the nations are in an uproar, the kingdoms totter" (vv. 2, 6). Other psalms of trust speak of such threats as the presence of enemies that threaten (23:5; 42:1–4), the reality of death (16:10), the dangers of war (27:3), the hazards of disease (91:6), or the perils found in nature (121:5–6). Indeed, much of the power of these poems is found in how surprisingly realistic they are about the genuine threats and dangers that a person encounters in life. Far from being naive, these psalms understand that humans live vulnerable lives and are at risk on any number of fronts. But by naming the very real perils of life, these psalms offer those who recite them the courage to face these threats squarely.

### The Language (Part 2): Expressions of Trust

Like the prayers for help, the psalms of trust express confidence in the Lord's providence. But unlike the prayers for help, in the songs of trust these expressions have become the dominant melody. These psalms express confidence by means of such phrases as "I shall not want" (23:1), "Whom shall I fear?" (27:1), "I shall not be moved" (16:8), "I trust" (52:8), and "I have calmed and quieted my soul" (131:2).

---

### PSALM 23 AS "ROD AND STAFF"

Take a moment and read Psalm 23.

The genre of Psalm 23 is often given to be a psalm of trust, which may be characterized as the "opposite," in terms of emphasis, of the prayer for help.

In the Western film *Rooster Cogburn* (1975), starring John Wayne and Katharine Hepburn, Eula Goodnight (played by Hepburn) quotes Psalm 23. In the face of menacing criminals passing through the village where she is a teacher, Goodnight answers the threat of violence, not with threats of her own but with the words of Psalm 23. Here recitation of the text functions as a shield and turns the villains aside. The scene represents the trust of Psalm 23 in an extreme sense. Now, compare the use of the psalm in the film *Pale Rider* (see the sidebar "A Restructuring of Psalm 23 in *Pale Rider*" in chap. 1). There, Psalm 23 is engaged out of a sense that trust is not reasonable, perhaps not even possible. The use of the psalm of trust is to express the need for help.

Identifying a psalm's genre does not put an end to our understanding and use of it.

---

### *The Language (Part 3): Descriptions of God's Care*

On what basis are the singers of these psalms able to express trust and confidence in the face of real and present danger? These poems manifest a remarkably uniform answer to this question: the presence of God. Psalm 46 says, "The LORD of hosts is with us" (vv. 7, 11). Psalm 23 says, "You are with me" (v. 4). Psalm 16 says, "The LORD [is] always before me" (v. 8). The consistent message in these psalms is confidence in the *active and effective presence of God*. The psalms describe God's presence in two different ways. On the one hand, the psalms offer a rich array of *metaphors that express the presence of God*. On the other hand, these poems describe *God's characteristic actions that God takes in the world*.

Much of the power in the psalms of trust is located in the metaphors that express the presence of God. For example, the psalms describe God as "shepherd" (23:1), banquet host (23:5), "light" (27:1), "shelter" (27:5), "my chosen portion and cup" (16:5; here "portion" means "inheritance"), "refuge" (46:1), "my rock" and "my fortress" (62:2), "a strong tower" (61:3), a "dwelling place" (90:1), a "keeper" (121:5; here "keeper" means "guardian"), "like . . . a mother" (131:2),[13] and so on. William Brown has written extensively about the theology and meaning of the psalms' metaphors. Describing the

---

13. Although the psalm does not explicitly say that the Lord is like a mother, it does make the connection between the comfort that a child receives from the mother and the calm that the

imaginative power of the metaphors, he has argued persuasively that "it is precisely the psalmist's deployment of metaphor that enables the personal language of pathos to be felt by readers of every generation."[14] These metaphors should not be thought of as secondary elements of the psalms of trust but rather should be understood as primary aspects of these psalms. The metaphors are not decorations that adorn the limbs of the tree: they are part of the tree itself. What metaphors—ancient or modern—communicate strength and assurance for you?

The other way in which the psalms of trust describe God's presence is by means of a series of phrases in which the psalms concretely express the Lord's characteristic activities. In many cases, these phrases extend the logic of the metaphors that are central to the psalms. For example, in Psalm 23 the Lord is first named as "my shepherd," and then the Lord is described as the one who "leads me beside still waters" and "leads me in right paths" (vv. 2–3). According to the psalms of trust, some of the characteristic activities of the Lord include giving "counsel" and instruction (16:7), delivering from enemies (27:2–5), providing shelter amid natural disaster and war (Ps. 46), and the like. Psalm 91 offers an uninhibited, soaring description of God's rescuing actions:

> You will tread on the lion and the adder,
>   the young lion and the serpent you will trample under foot.
>
> Those who love me, I will deliver;
>   I will protect those who know my name.
> When they call to me, I will answer them;
>   I will be with them in trouble,
>   I will rescue them and honor them.
> With long life I will satisfy them,
>   and show them my salvation. (vv. 13–16)

In seeking to understand these extravagant phrases, we recognize that the promises here are not to be interpreted in some naive, rigid sense. That is, Psalm 91 does not literally promise that those who trust in God can step on poisonous snakes and survive (v. 13). Nor does the psalm promise that all faithful people automatically are granted long lives (v. 16). As noted above, these psalms are quite honest about the genuine threats and dangers that confront all who live in a broken world. Rather, these sentences are general

---

psalmist has experienced from God. On this basis, the psalm goes on to say that Israel should "hope in the LORD" (131:3).

14. William P. Brown, *Seeing the Psalms: A Theology of Metaphor* (Louisville: Westminster John Knox, 2002), 3.

## STRANGE SORTS OF SONGS

Perhaps you imagine that the biblical songs were always sung with great reverence and sincerity, by very pious people. The actual case, however, is far different. Sarcasm is not a recent invention. And the truth is that the Bible tells of a special group of singers who specialized in singing sarcastic songs. These people were generally known as *the prophets*.

For example, the prophet Amos, in chapter 5 of the book that is named after him, sings a sarcastic "lament" (also called a funeral dirge). Here are the words:

Hear this word, Israel, this lament I take up concerning you:

"Fallen is Virgin Israel,
    never to rise again,
deserted in her own land,
    with no one to lift her up."
This is what the Sovereign LORD says to Israel:
"Your city that marches out a thousand strong
    will have only a hundred left;
your town that marches out a hundred strong
    will have only ten left." (Amos 5:1–3 NIV)

In this song, Amos was aping the musical form of the funeral dirge. He laid his hands on this sacred form in order to announce to the people of Israel (here called "Virgin Israel") that they are already dead in their sins.

Similarly, the prophet Isaiah borrows the form of the "love song." In the love songs of ancient Israel, the beloved object of the singer's affection is often pictured as a garden (cf. the love songs in the Song of Songs).

I will sing for the one I love
    a song about his vineyard:
My loved one had a vineyard
    on a fertile hillside.
He dug it up and cleared it of stones
    and planted it with the choicest vines.
He built a watchtower in it
    and cut out a winepress as well.
Then he looked for a crop of good grapes,
    but it yielded only bad fruit.
"Now you dwellers in Jerusalem and people of Judah,
    judge between me and my vineyard.
What more could have been done for my vineyard
    than I have done for it?
When I looked for good grapes,
    why did it yield only bad?
Now I will tell you
    what I am going to do to my vineyard:

> I will take away its hedge,
>     and it will be destroyed;
> I will break down its wall,
>     and it will be trampled.
> I will make it a wasteland,
>     neither pruned nor cultivated,
>     and briers and thorns will grow there.
> I will command the clouds
>     not to rain on it."
> The vineyard of the LORD Almighty
>     is the nation of Israel,
> and the people of Judah
>     are the vines he delighted in.
> And he looked for justice,
>     but saw bloodshed;
> for righteousness,
>     but heard cries of distress. (Isa. 5:1–7 NIV)

Understanding these prophetic critiques would have required the prophets' ancient audiences first to recognize the forms of these songs—a dirge and a love song—and second to realize that the forms were being sung sarcastically. How do you imagine the ancient audiences reacted to these sarcastic uses of sacred forms?

descriptions of the type of saving help that God provides *in the midst of life's dangers*. Just as the psalms of trust do not deny the real risks in life, they do not promise universal protection for the faithful. Rather, these sentences are "sketches" of what God's delivering power looks like. They offer *symbolic descriptions* of God's activity. Rather than offering naive promises that force a person to deny life's threats, they are expressions of trust as the psalmists face life's dangers critically and at the same time rely on the presence of the divine.

## "Thank You! Thank You! Thank You!"—Songs of Thanksgiving

A final genre of psalm is called the song of thanksgiving. The song of thanksgiving shares some aspects in common with the hymn of praise and some aspects in common with the prayer for help.

### The Situation and Audiences of the Song of Thanksgiving

Similar to the hymn of praise, these songs tell who God is by telling what God has done. Also similar to the hymn of praise, the songs of thanksgiving are usually addressed both to God and to a human audience. With respect to the hymn of praise, it may be recalled that at times the praise of God is spoken to God directly in the second person ("You, O LORD . . .") and at other times is spoken about God in the third person ("The LORD is gracious . . ."). Most of the songs of thanksgiving include both of these types of praise. The songs of thanksgiving also share some things in common with prayers for help. Similar to prayers for help, these songs seem to be sung in relation to a specific experience of crisis; but whereas the prayers for help are spoken in the midst of a crisis, the songs of thanksgiving are sung *after the crisis has passed*. In these songs, the singer looks back and narrates the experience of passing through a crisis. Also similar to the prayer for help, the song of thanksgiving may be spoken by an individual (for example, Ps. 30) who has passed through a crisis or by a community (for example, Ps. 66) that has passed through a crisis.

Psalm 30 offers an excellent example of the song of thanksgiving—in this case, the song of an individual who has survived a crisis.[15]

> [1] I will extol you, O LORD, for you have drawn me up,
>> and did not let my foes rejoice over me.
> [2] O LORD my God, I cried to you for help,
>> and you have healed me.
> [3] O LORD, you brought up my soul from Sheol,
>> restored me to life from among those gone down to the Pit.
>
> [4] Sing praises to the LORD, O you his faithful ones,
>> and give thanks to his holy name.
> [5] For his anger is but for a moment;
>> his favor is for a lifetime.
> Weeping may linger for the night,
>> but joy comes with the morning.
>
> [6] As for me, I said in my prosperity,
>> "I shall never be moved."
> [7] By your favor, O LORD,
>> you had established me as a strong mountain;
> you hid your face;
>> I was dismayed.
>
> [8] To you, O LORD, I cried,
>> and to the LORD I made supplication:
> [9] "What profit is there in my death,
>> if I go down to the Pit?

15. Other psalms often categorized as songs of thanksgiving include 9; 18; 32; 34; 40; 57; 66; 75; 92; 107; 116; 118; 138.

Will the dust praise you?
  Will it tell of your faithfulness?
[10] Hear, O Lord, and be gracious to me!
  O Lord, be my helper!"

[11] You have turned my mourning into dancing;
  you have taken off my sackcloth and clothed me with joy,
[12] so that my soul may praise you and not be silent.
  O Lord my God, I will give thanks to you forever.

One of the most helpful ways to approach the songs of thanksgiving is to understand them as the "second chapter" in a two-chapter story—with the prayer for help being chapter 1. The reader may recall that in the prayer for help, the petitioner (1) is in the midst of a crisis, (2) calls on God and requests God's saving help, and (3) promises to praise God once God's help has arrived. In the song of thanksgiving (chapter 2 of the story), the singer (1) looks back on the time of crisis, (2) describes how God provided help, and (3) offers the praise that was promised.

| Chapter 1—Prayer for Help | Chapter 2—Song of Thanksgiving |
|---|---|
| In the crisis → | Recalls crisis |
| Requests help → | Describes help received |
| Promises praise → | Delivers praise |

In Psalm 30, these characteristic elements of the song of thanksgiving are evident: a report of a crisis, description of the help that was received, and the delivery of praise (in a threefold form, see below).

### The Language (Part 1): Report of Crisis and Request for Help

Just as the various prayers for help are voiced from a range of different crises, the songs of thanksgiving reflect the experience of those who have passed through a range of crises: there is no one type of crisis that is reflected in the songs of thanksgiving. Indeed, just as the prayers for help seem to use generic and symbolic language for their crises, so that individuals in many different types of crises can pray those prayers, so also the songs of thanksgiving tend to use metaphorical language for past crises, in order to make these songs available to many different people. In Psalm 30 the past crisis is alluded to with a variety of different images: the oppression of "foes [who] rejoice over me" (v. 1), the experience of nearly going "down to the Pit" (v. 3), the sense of suffering from God's "anger" and of "weeping . . . [throughout] the night" (v. 5), the feeling that God "hid [God's] face" (v. 7), and the image of being in "mourning" and clothed in "sackcloth" (v. 11; "sackcloth" here is the way people either repented of sin or expressed grief). This bewildering array of metaphors may seem less than perfectly consistent. Yet the language is not intended to describe one situation and one situation only but rather to evoke a range of possible crises. In other songs of thanksgiving, the past crises are described with such rich language as "The cords of death encompassed me; the torrents of perdition assailed me" (18:4), "My body wasted away, . . . my strength was dried up" (32:3–4), my feet were stuck in "a miry bog" (40:2), "We went through fire and through water" (66:12), and so on.

Essential to the description of the crisis is the psalmist's report of asking God for help. In Psalm 30, the singer says, "I cried to you for help" (v. 2), and reports, "To you, O Lord, I cried, and to the Lord I made supplication" (v. 8). Psalm 107 is a more generic and longer psalm that describes four different types of people who were in crisis: those who "wandered in desert wastes" (v. 4), prisoners who "sat in darkness and in gloom" (v. 10), those who "were sick" (v. 17), and travelers who "went down to the sea in ships" (v. 23). Then it describes how each type of people "cried to the Lord in their trouble" (vv. 6, 13, 19, 28).

### The Language (Part 2): Description of Help Received

Perhaps it would be fair to say that the heart that beats at the center of the song of thanksgiving is the report of the help the singer received. The singers of these psalms want the listeners to know that saving help is available for those who cry "to the Lord in their trouble." In Psalm 30, the help is again described in a number of ways—as being "drawn" up, "healed" (vv. 1–2), "restored . . . to life" (v. 3), and, in a wonderfully imaginative phrase, as being "clothed . . . with joy" (v. 11). In other psalms, similarly evocative imagery is used.

### The Language (Part 3): Praise Delivered

While the heart of the song of thanksgiving is the report of the help that was received, the praise that these psalms deliver is the way in which they express their "thanksgiving." In fact, the Hebrew language of the Old Testament does not have a word that means "thanks" or "thanksgiving." The word that is often translated as "thanks"—as in Psalm 107:1, "O give thanks to the Lord"—actually means something more like "testify" or "confess" or "make known."[16] To put it loosely, rather than saying thank you to God,

---

16. See, for example, Westermann, *The Psalms*, 72; and John Goldingay, *Psalms 1–41*, vol. 1 of *Psalms* (Grand Rapids: Baker Academic, 2006), 592.

these psalms express their gratitude by telling others what God has done. The sort of gratitude that God desires is not a private thank-you note but a public testimony of praise (and remember, praise is telling others who God is by telling what God has done).

In the psalms of thanksgiving, the praise is usually expressed in a threefold way. First, these psalms often begin with an expression of praise. For example, Psalm 107 starts out, "O give thanks to the LORD, for he is good," and Psalm 30 begins, "I will extol you, O LORD." Second, in the middle of these psalms, there is usually a call for others to join in praise. So in Psalm 30:4, the psalmist calls on the gathered community, "Sing praises to the LORD, O you his faithful ones." In Psalm 66:8, the psalmist implores the congregation, "Bless our God, O peoples, let the sound of his praise be heard." Notice how this is a little different from the hymn of praise since in the hymn the call to praise usually starts the song. In the song of thanksgiving, it comes in the middle, after the psalmist has narrated the personal experience of deliverance. Third, in these psalms, the singer's song modulates at some point from narrating what God has done to describing who God is and what God is like. That is, after reporting individual experience, the singer usually shifts gears and describes God's character: ˙

> For his anger is but for a moment;
>     his favor is for a lifetime.
> Weeping may linger for the night,
>     but joy comes with the morning. (30:5)

## Conclusion

In this chapter the reader was introduced to the concept of genre. It was argued that understanding the genre of a piece of writing is critical to understanding it. The reader was also introduced to the view that within the psalms are two types of genres: those that are classified according to their common "forms" and those that are classified according to common "themes" or "content." Finally, in this chapter, the reader was introduced to examples of four psalm genres that are classified according to common "forms": (1) prayers for help, (2) hymns of praise, (3) psalms of trust, and (4) songs of thanksgiving. In the next chapter the reader will be introduced to those genres that are classified according to common thematic content.

---

## GOING DEEPER

In order to deepen your understanding of the genres of the psalms and how they work, consider doing one or more of the following activities:

1. Imagine a crisis time in your life when you felt either frightened or confident in the midst of that crisis. Read either Psalm 13 (a prayer for help) or Psalm 23 (a psalm of trust) and try to imagine how well or poorly the psalm would have fit your life in that time of crisis.

2. Following the form of a prayer for help, a hymn of praise, a psalm of trust, or a song of thanksgiving, write your own psalm that expresses your own emotions and thoughts.

3. Open up a Bible and find Psalm 3 and Psalm 95. Identify which type of psalm you think these psalms are and label different elements of the psalms.

---

## FOR FURTHER READING

Brueggemann, Walter. *The Psalms and the Life of Faith*. Minneapolis: Fortress, 1995.

DeClaissé-Walford, Nancy. *Introduction to the Psalms*. St. Louis: Chalice, 2004.

McCann, J. Clinton. *A Theological Introduction to the Book of Psalms*. Nashville: Abingdon, 1993.

Miller, Patrick D. *Interpreting the Psalms*. Philadelphia: Fortress, 1986.

# THREE

# What Is a Psalm?

*Learning to Understand*
*Different Psalm Genres—Part 2*

## Reintroducing the Concept of Genre

In chapter 2, the reader was introduced to the concept of genre in general, and more specifically to the concept of genre in the psalms. It was argued that understanding the genre of a piece of literature is critical to understanding it. Indeed, if one misunderstands the genre of a given piece of literature, one is likely to misunderstand the meaning of a document's words. *The competent reader of the psalms is able to identify what genre of the psalms a particular psalm is, which better enables the reader to understand the meaning of the words that occur in that psalm.*

The reader was also introduced to the view that within the psalms are two general sets of genres:

- genres classified according to their common "forms" (see chap. 2); and
- genres classified according to common "themes" or "content" (introduced in this chapter).

A wit once remarked that if you put two academic scholars in a room and ask them a question, you will get three different opinions. The point of this joke is that people whose work is to deal with ideas are, to use a metaphor, making distinctions between different shades of gray. And different scholars will draw the line between different shades in slightly different places. So when it comes to psalm genres that are classified according to thematic content, if you ask two psalms scholars for a list, you may get three different lists. But here is our list:

- Royal psalms have to do with Israel's human king.
- Enthronement psalms have to do with God as Israel's king.
- Wisdom psalms draw on Israel's wisdom tradition and seek to teach something to the reader (or audience).
- Creation psalms speak of God as creator and the earth as God's creation.
- Historical psalms retell part of Israel's history.
- Zion psalms speak about Jerusalem (and specifically about the temple) as the place where God abides.
- Imprecatory psalms ask God to punish those who oppress the psalmist or the psalmist's community.
- Penitential psalms ask for forgiveness.
- Liturgical psalms give directions for a worship ritual.

The reader may recall that in the previous chapter the sections devoted to each of the genres included subsections about the situation and the language of the various genres. The reason for that was precisely because those "formal genres" are defined by the fact that they contain consistent types of language and fit in specific types of social settings. This chapter lacks those subsections. Why? As the reader may have already guessed, it is precisely because this chapter introduces those genres that are defined by their *common themes* rather than common language. For the most part, these genres lack consistent language (an exception is the "enthronement psalms").

## "It's Good to Have a King"—Royal Psalms

Consider the following sections of four different psalms. In what ways are these poems similar? In what ways are these poems different?

### Psalm 21

The king rejoices in your strength, LORD.
How great is his joy in the victories you give!
You have granted him his heart's desire
and have not withheld the request of his lips. (vv. 1–2 NIV)

### Psalm 89

But you have rejected, you have spurned,
you have been very angry with your anointed one.
You have renounced the covenant with your servant
and have defiled his crown in the dust. (vv. 38–39 NIV)

### Psalm 72

Endow the king with your justice, O God,
the royal son with your righteousness.
May he judge your people in righteousness,
your afflicted ones with justice. (vv. 1–2 NIV)

### Psalm 20

Now this I know: The LORD gives victory to his anointed.
He answers him from his heavenly sanctuary
with the victorious power of his right hand.
Some trust in chariots and some in horses,
but we trust in the name of the LORD our God. (vv. 6–7 NIV)

Now, answer this question: What kinds of psalms are these four poems?

On the one hand, these psalms are all different. If we are thinking about the "forms" of the psalms that we introduced in chapter 2, the four psalms are different. Psalm 21 is a song of thanksgiving: it gives thanks for what God has done for the king. Psalm 89 is a prayer for help / lament psalm: it cries out in pain on behalf of the king, who has suffered some sort of crisis. Psalm 72 is also a prayer for help, but rather than praying for rescue, this psalm prays for guidance so that the king will govern well. Psalm 20 is a psalm of trust: it expresses confidence on behalf of the king in the midst of a crisis.

On the other hand, these psalms are all the same. If one is thinking thematically, these psalms are all about ancient Israel's king. For this reason, they are called royal psalms.

The royal psalms of the Psalter deal thematically with Israel's human king.[1] In spite of the fact that these psalms exhibit neither a "fixed literary

---

1. Scholars differ as to which psalms they categorize as royal psalms. Here is our list: 2; 18; 20; 21; 45; 72; 89; 101; 110; 132; 144.

pattern"[2] nor a consistent life setting or audience, they are nevertheless recognized by most scholars as a genre. The reason for this is that the psalms demonstrate a consistent thematic focus on the king. It is clear that these psalms thus share a context: they were composed for one or another event related to the life of the king.[3] Moreover, it is clear that the ancient psalmists themselves recognized the royal psalms as a genre of psalms. One reason for this conclusion is that editors who arranged the final form of the Psalter placed royal psalms at key places in the collection: the very fact that the psalms were placed in specific places shows that the editors thought of them as a group.[4] Another reason for this conclusion is that the poet who penned Psalm 45 begins with the words, "My heart is astir with gracious words; I speak my poem to a king" (v. 1 NJPS). As the German scholar Hans-Joachim Kraus has suggested, the phrase "poem to a king" (Hebrew: *ma'asay lemelek*) refers to a *royal psalm—a poem to or about the king.*[5]

Psalm 72 is a good example of a royal psalm. The psalm begins thus:

> Endow the king with your justice, O God,
>   the royal son with your righteousness.
> May he judge your people in righteousness,
>   your afflicted ones with justice.
>
> May the mountains bring prosperity to the people,
>   the hills the fruit of righteousness.
> May he defend the afflicted among the people
>   and save the children of the needy;
>   may he crush the oppressor. (vv. 1–4 NIV)

Notice that this psalm is both a prayer for help and a royal psalm. According to its formal patterns, it is a prayer: its audience is God, it is filled with imperative requests for help, and so on (see discussion of prayers for help in chap. 2). According to its thematic content, however, it is a royal psalm: it is about the king. The psalm calls on God to grant the king the qualities of justice and righteousness so that he may fulfill his royal duties well. To be

2. William P. Brown, "Psalms, Book of," in *The New Interpreter's Dictionary of the Bible*, ed. Katherine Doob Sakenfeld (Nashville: Abingdon, 2009), 4:666.

3. See Hermann Gunkel, *Introduction to the Psalms: The Genres of the Religious Lyric of Israel*, completed by Joachim Begrich, trans. James D. Nogalski (Macon, GA: Mercer University Press, 1998), 99.

4. See Gerald Wilson, "The Use of the Royal Psalms at the 'Seams' of the Hebrew Psalter," *Journal for the Study of the Old Testament* 35 (1986): 85–94.

5. Hans-Joachim Kraus, *Psalms 1–59: A Commentary*, trans. Hilton C. Oswald (trans. of 5th German ed., 1978; Minneapolis: Augsburg, 1988), 56.

specific, the psalm has in mind the king's role as a mediator of disputes (see, for example, the stories of Kings David and Solomon in "judging" specific disputes in 2 Sam. 15:1–6 and 1 Kings 3:16–28).

Other royal psalms follow a similar pattern. In terms of form, they fit one of the formal genres (such as a prayer for help, a worship liturgy, or a song of praise). In terms of content, they deal with a specific role that the king played or a specific moment in the life of the king. A few examples of other royal psalms include these:

Psalm 2. A worship liturgy, likely composed for a new king's coronation.

Psalm 18. A song of thanksgiving, likely composed to give thanks after the king had experienced delivery from a crisis. In this regard, note that the same psalm also occurs in 2 Samuel 22, where David sings the psalm "on the day when the Lord delivered him from the hand of all his enemies, and from the hand of Saul" (v. 1).

Psalm 20. A prayer for the king, likely prayed before the king led the Israelite army into battle.

Psalm 21. A song of thanksgiving, likely composed after the king had experienced a military victory or had some similar experience of deliverance.

Psalm 45. A hymn of praise, likely composed for the king's wedding.

Psalm 89. This psalm combines a song of praise and a prayer for help. The first half (vv. 1–37) praises God for the divine faithfulness shown to King David and his descendants. The second half (vv. 38–51), which may have been composed after the king had experienced a serious defeat such as the destruction of Jerusalem in 586 BCE, is a prayer for help that calls on God to be faithful.

One of the interesting aspects of the royal psalms is to note that all of them were surely composed while Israel still had a monarchy, thus sometime before the year 586 BCE, when Jerusalem was destroyed and the last Davidic king was taken into exile in Babylon. But the book of Psalms was not collected into its final form until many years later, perhaps as late as 100 CE.[6] These psalms about Davidic kings were originally written to bear witness to how God works through human beings, especially through leaders such as kings. But why were they included in the Psalter so many years after the

---

6. The date of the formation of the Psalter is debated. See Gerald Wilson, "A First-Century C.E. Date for the Closing of the Psalter?," in *Haim M. I. Gevaryahu: Memorial Volume*, ed. Joshua J. Adler (Jerusalem: World Jewish Bible Center, 1990), 136–43.

Davidic monarchy had ceased? Because, as Claus Westermann wrote, "they bear witness to messianic expectations."[7] They were retained because the community believed that God would keep the promises that these psalms contain—promises about a coming king, a coming "Messiah" (to use the Hebrew term), a coming "Christ" (to use the Greek term).

## "Meet the New Boss, Same as the Old Boss"—Enthronement Psalms

In the following psalms, notice that a key phrase is repeated:

> God reigns over the nations,
>> God is seated on his holy throne. (47:8 NIV)

> The LORD reigns, he is robed in majesty;
>> The LORD is robed in majesty and armed with strength. (93:1 NIV)

> Say among the nations, "The LORD reigns."
>> The world is firmly established, it cannot be moved;
>> he will judge the peoples with equity. (96:10 NIV)

> The LORD reigns, let the earth be glad;
>> let the distant shores rejoice. (97:1 NIV)

> The LORD reigns,
>> let the nations tremble;
> he sits enthroned between the cherubim,
>> let the earth shake. (99:1 NIV)

All of the above psalms have a common phrase: "The LORD reigns" (or "God reigns"). Other translations render this phrase as "The LORD is king" or "The LORD has become king."[8] These psalms picture God as "enthroned" on high and reigning over the entire earth. For that reason, these psalms are known as the enthronement psalms.

Psalm 93 exemplifies the genre:

> [1] The LORD is king, he is robed in majesty;
>> the LORD is robed, he is girded with strength.

7. Claus Westermann, *The Psalms: Structure, Content, and Message* (Minneapolis: Augsburg, 1980), 106.

8. See Sigmund Mowinckel, *The Psalms in Israel's Worship*, 2 vols. (Nashville: Abingdon, 1962), 1:107; and James Luther Mays, *The Lord Reigns: A Theological Handbook to the Psalms* (Louisville: Westminster John Knox, 1994), 12–15.

He has established the world; it shall never be moved;
   ²your throne is established from of old;
   you are from everlasting.

³The floods have lifted up, O LORD,
   the floods have lifted up their voice;
   the floods lift up their roaring.
⁴More majestic than the thunders of mighty waters,
   more majestic than the waves of the sea,
   majestic on high is the LORD!

⁵Your decrees are very sure;
   holiness befits your house,
   O LORD, forevermore.

Typical of this group of psalms, the poem begins with the shout, "The LORD is king!" Psalms 97 and 99 also begin with this exclamation. In Psalms 47; 96; and 98, this cry occurs elsewhere in the psalm (47:8; 96:10; 98:6). Psalm 95 does not have the exact phrase, but it does say, "The LORD is a great God, and a great King above all gods" (v. 3). Note here that these psalms do share this basic common language.

In addition to this main thematic link, these psalms also share several other characteristics, both thematic and formal. Thematically, the psalms call for global worship of and submission to God as the universal ruler. The psalms link God's rule of the universe to the divine act of creation. Why is God king? Because God has created and maintains all: "The sea is his, for he made it, and the dry land, which his hands have formed" (95:5). Throughout these psalms, aspects of creation are personified—the sea, the land, the floods, the heavens, the field, the world, the hills, the trees of the forest, and so on—and all are called on to worship and submit to the Lord. The Lord's role as lawgiver (93:5) and judge (95:8–11; 96:13; 99:4) are also a thread that runs through these psalms. Other psalms, such as 48 and 114 to name just two, also share certain aspects of these psalms but are usually not numbered among the enthronement psalms.

Psalms scholar Sigmund Mowinckel theorized that the enthronement psalms were performed during a fall worship festival that celebrated both the harvest and the new year.⁹ He argued that in these psalms the shout "The LORD has become king!" functioned in a way that was similar to how the

---

9. See Mowinckel, *Psalms in Israel's Worship*, vol. 1, chap. 5. In ancient Israel, as is still the case in modern Rabbinic Judaism, the new year (Hebrew: *Rosh-hashanah*) was celebrated in autumn.

shout "Christ is risen!" was used by Christians each year at Easter to com-
memorate the resurrection of Jesus. Mowinckel proposed that we understand
the enthronement psalms as having been used at this New Year's Festival to
"salute Yahweh as the king, who has just ascended his royal throne to wield
his royal power."[10] While Mowinckel's line of interpretation is not widely
followed, he did nevertheless succeed in isolating the enthronement psalms
as a defined group of psalms. The fact that, with the exception of Psalm 47,
all of them are tightly grouped together in the Psalter (93; 95–99) further
suggests that the ancient editors of the Psalter saw them as a defined genre.

In a sense, these psalms provide a theological counterbalance to the royal
psalms. The royal psalms emphasize human kings and leaders as channels
through which God acts on behalf of the chosen people. Those psalms describe the God who draws near and takes action through human agents. The
enthronement psalms, on the other hand, emphasize the God who is completely other, who alone is King, who transcends all of creation and therefore
is to be worshiped and praised by all.

## "Everything I Needed to Know, I Learned from the Psalms"—
## Wisdom (Instructional) Psalms

Read the following phrases and try to imagine what type of person would
speak these words or where you have heard similar sayings:

> Do not fret because of the wicked;
>     do not be envious of wrongdoers,
> for they will soon fade like the grass,
>     and wither like the green herb. (37:1–2)

> Happy are those who consider the poor;
>     the LORD delivers them in the day of trouble. (41:1)

> When we look at the wise, they die;
>     fool and dolt perish together
>     and leave their wealth to others. (49:10)

> The law of the LORD is perfect,
>     reviving the soul;
> the decrees of the LORD are sure,
>     making wise the simple. (19:7)

---

10. Mowinckel, *Psalms in Israel's Worship*, 106.

What sort of person comes to mind who would say things such as these? A teacher? A grandparent? A coach or mentor? If you imagined the speaker of these verses as someone in the range of a teacher or a wizened elder, then you are in the same company as many psalms scholars. These verses come from a group of psalms known either as wisdom psalms or instructional psalms.

Wisdom psalms are those poems that bear the mark of Israel's wisdom tradition (the influence of Israel's wisdom tradition on the Bible is most clear in the three wisdom books in the Old Testament: Proverbs, Ecclesiastes, and Job). Different scholars define the category of wisdom psalm in different ways, which then leads those scholars to include different psalms in their lists of wisdom psalms.[11] For the sake of this book, we are defining a wisdom psalm as a poem that includes these features:

1. *Teaching tone.* These psalms speak in an instructional manner. As one leading scholar of the wisdom psalms has written, "The canonical wisdom psalms predominantly direct their discourse horizontally toward humankind, not vertically toward the deity. They are the products of teacher poets intent on imparting their lessons on the good life to those who thirst for understanding."[12] Psalm 78 even explicitly begins, "Give ear, O my people, to my *teaching*" (emphasis added).

2. *Wisdom terminology.* These psalms exhibit a high concentration of the vocabulary that occurs in other Old Testament wisdom literature (Proverbs, Ecclesiastes, Job). There is no one term or set of terms that occurs in every wisdom psalm. Nor does the occurrence of a term in a psalm automatically mean that it is a wisdom psalm. But the concentration of certain terms helps flag a poem as a wisdom psalm. These terms include words such as the Hebrew word *'ashrey*, which is normally translated as "Happy are those who . . ." (Ps. 1:1) or "Blessed is the one who . . ." (1:1 NIV). Other examples of typical wisdom terminology include contrasting pairs of terms, such as "the righteous" and "the wicked" (1:6; 37:17), and references to God's "way" (1:6; 37:34) and "counsel" (73:24).

11. The category of wisdom psalms is much debated by scholars, as is the list of which psalms should be included under this heading. Among the psalms often included are 1; 19; 32; 34; 37; 39; 49; 73; 78; 112; 119; 127; 128; and 133. Often Pss. 1; 19; and 119 are further defined as "Torah psalms" because they refer specifically to the Lord's "Torah." For a discussion of the category "wisdom psalm," see J. Kenneth Kuntz, "Reclaiming Biblical Wisdom Psalms: A Response to Crenshaw," *Currents in Biblical Research* 1, no. 2 (2003): 145–54.

12. Kuntz, "Reclaiming Biblical Wisdom Psalms," 151.

3. *Wisdom questions or topics.* These psalms ask questions or pursue themes similar to those tackled in the other wisdom books. Psalm 1, for example, takes up the theme of the best "path" or "way" in life (as in Prov. 3:31; 4:11). Psalm 73 (see below) takes up the question of why evildoers seem to prosper while good people suffer; compare this with the book of Job, which tells the story of a righteous man who suffers.

Psalm 73 is a good example of a wisdom psalm:

> [1] Truly God is good to [Israel],[13]
>   to those who are pure in heart.
> [2] But as for me, my feet had almost stumbled;
>   my steps had nearly slipped.
> [3] For I was envious of the arrogant;
>   I saw the prosperity of the wicked.
>
> [4] For they have no pain;
>   their bodies are sound and sleek.
> [5] They are not in trouble as others are;
>   they are not plagued like other people.
> [6] Therefore pride is their necklace;
>   violence covers them like a garment.
> [7] Their eyes swell out with fatness;
>   their hearts overflow with follies.
> [8] They scoff and speak with malice;
>   loftily they threaten oppression.
> [9] They set their mouths against heaven,
>   and their tongues range over the earth.
>
> [10] Therefore the people turn and praise them,
>   and find no fault in them.
> [11] And they say, "How can God know?
>   Is there knowledge in the Most High?"
> [12] Such are the wicked;
>   always at ease, they increase in riches.
> [13] All in vain I have kept my heart clean
>   and washed my hands in innocence.
> [14] For all day long I have been plagued,
>   and am punished every morning.

13. The NRSV changes "Israel" to "the upright," but we prefer to retain "Israel," as most translations do.

¹⁵ If I had said, "I will talk on in this way,"
      I would have been untrue to the circle of your children.
¹⁶ But when I thought how to understand this,
      it seemed to me a wearisome task,
¹⁷ until I went into the sanctuary of God;
      then I perceived their end.
¹⁸ Truly you set them in slippery places;
      you make them fall to ruin.
¹⁹ How they are destroyed in a moment,
      swept away utterly by terrors!
²⁰ They are like a dream when one awakes;
      on awaking you despise their phantoms.

²¹ When my soul was embittered,
      when I was pricked in heart,
²² I was stupid and ignorant;
      I was like a brute beast toward you.
²³ Nevertheless I am continually with you;
      you hold my right hand.
²⁴ You guide me with your counsel,
      and afterward you will receive me with honor.
²⁵ Whom have I in heaven but you?
      And there is nothing on earth that I desire other than you.
²⁶ My flesh and my heart may fail,
      but God is the strength of my heart and my portion forever.

²⁷ Indeed, those who are far from you will perish;
      you put an end to those who are false to you.
²⁸ But for me it is good to be near God;
      I have made the Lord GOD my refuge,
      to tell of all your works.

The psalm displays the above-defined thematic features of a typical wisdom psalm. The poem takes up the difficult theological issue of why good things happen to bad people ("the wicked," v. 3), while bad things seem to happen to God's people ("Israel," v. 1; or "the circle of your children," v. 15). As mentioned above, this theme is similar to the book of Job, in which one of the major themes is why a "blameless and upright" man suffers (Job 1:1). Psalm 73 pursues this question in verses 2–20. The psalmist talks about how the wicked "have no pain," "are not in trouble as others are," and while "always at ease, they increase in riches" (vv. 4, 5, 12). The poem talks about how it is tempting for people to adopt the moral choices of the wicked: "I was envious of the arrogant" (v. 3). In fact, the psalmist admits to having fallen for this temptation: "as for me, my feet had almost stumbled" (v. 2).

The tone of the poem is instructional. The psalm starts (in v. 1) with a teaching statement, which sounds like it could come right out of the book of Proverbs: "Truly God is good to Israel, to those who are pure in heart." Like many psalms, this poem speaks both in the third person, *about God*, and in the second person, *to God*. The first half of the poem (vv. 1–14) is spoken to God in an instructional tone. In the second half of the poem (vv. 15–28), the speech shifts to more prayer-like talk to God. The poem now functions both as prayer and as instruction. For example, the psalm affirms some of the central teachings of the Old Testament. It affirms the presence of God: "I am continually with you; you hold my right hand" (v. 23). The psalm teaches that the lifestyle of the wicked may avail in the short run, but in the long run to choose evil is to sow the seeds of one's own demise: "Truly you set them in slippery places; you make them fall to ruin" (v. 18). The psalm affirms that God's guidance and protection are made available through God's Word: "You guide me with your counsel, and afterward you will receive me with honor" (v. 24). As one prominent psalms scholar wrote of the instructional function of the poem, "Psalm 73 reinforces the essential instruction already offered in Psalms 1–72: God reigns; we belong to God; no experience separates us from God; happiness or goodness means to live in dependence not upon oneself but by taking refuge in God."[14]

Moreover, the vocabulary remains similar to that found in wisdom literature. To cite just one example, the psalmist says, "But when I thought how to understand this, it seemed to me a wearisome task" (v. 16). Note how similar this is to the language of the book of Ecclesiastes: "So I turned my mind to understand, to investigate and to search out wisdom and the scheme of things" (Eccles. 7:25 NIV); and "all things are wearisome[,] more than one can express" (Eccles. 1:8).

### "How Majestic Is Your Name in All the Earth"—Creation Psalms

Psalms scholars also often speak of a group of psalms known as creation psalms. Like the other psalms described in this chapter, these psalms do not share a common form but do share a common theme: God as loving creator and all of the universe as God's beloved creation. Consider these passages:

> When I consider your heavens, the work of your fingers,
>     the moon and the stars, which you have set in place,

14. J. Clinton McCann, *A Theological Introduction to the Book of Psalms* (Nashville: Abingdon, 1993), 143.

what is mankind that you are mindful of them,
  human beings that you care for them? (8:3–4 NIV)

The heavens declare the glory of God;
  the skies proclaim the work of his hands.
Day after day they pour forth speech;
  night after night they reveal knowledge. (19:1–2 NIV)

For you created my inmost being;
  you knit me together in my mother's womb.
I praise you because I am fearfully and wonderfully made;
  your works are wonderful, I know that full well. (139:13–14 NIV)

Notice that these psalms share a common theme—God as creator and the creation as the work of a loving God—but also that each psalm is quite different. In Psalm 8, the singer realizes that creation is very large and then

## WHEN GOD WAITS AHEAD OF YOU

Alienation: from one's past, from other human beings, from faith, from a God whose knowledge and nature are "too wonderful" for us to comprehend (Ps. 139:6)—these issues are common to us all and are central to the Bible. One may think of Elijah's isolation, the cry of Jesus from the cross, and of course the desperate pleas of the authors of the psalms. The feeling of separation from God is the crossroads of faith, and it is a fundamental reality in life.

The biblical answer to this feeling of separation is, above all, the promise that "God is with you," that "God will pursue you," that "wherever you go, God will be there."

This biblical promise is echoed in the Showtime series *Penny Dreadful* (2014–16) by a most unlikely figure. *Penny Dreadful* is a story, at its core, about "alienation and dread."

"John Clare" (played by Rory Kinnear) is the pseudonym of "The Creature," Frankenstein's monster. In a moment of beautiful gentleness, Clare speaks hope to Vanessa Ives (played by Eva Green) in her despair: "No matter how far you have walked from God, he is still waiting ahead of you."

Or, as Psalm 139:8–10 puts it,

If I ascend to heaven, you are there;
  if I make my bed in Sheol, you are there.
If I take the wings of the morning
  and settle at the farthest limits of the sea,
even there your hand shall lead me,
  and your right hand shall hold me fast.

wonders, "In such a vast world, what does a single human being matter?" In Psalm 139, by contrast, the psalmist thinks about the miracle of life and speaks of the poet's body as carefully "knit . . . together" by God, and more, that God is present at all times and places in life. And in Psalm 19, the poet imagines creation as singing a wordless song of praise to God's glory.

Creation psalms include Psalms 8; 19; 65; 90; 104; 139; and 148.[15] In terms of form, creation psalms take the shape of one of the formal genres (such as a prayer for help, a worship liturgy, or a song of praise). In terms of content, they expand on one or more aspects of the theme of creation, as in these examples:

- Psalm 8 is a hymn of praise that expands on the special place of humanity in general within the vast and complex domain of creation.
- Psalm 139 is a prayer for help that focuses on the one praying as a unique, individual human being who was "fearfully and wonderfully made" (v. 14) and then asks God for protection from "the bloodthirsty" (v. 19).
- Psalm 104, the longest of the creation psalms, is a hymn of praise that speaks of God's ongoing role of sustaining and providing for creation.
- Psalms 19 and 148 are hymns of praise that poetically describe creation itself as praising God: "The heavens are telling the glory of God" (19:1) and "Praise him, sun and moon!" (148:3).
- Psalm 65 is a hymn of praise that focuses on the annual fall harvest as a sign of God's faithfulness: "You crown the year with your bounty. . . . The hills gird themselves with joy, the meadows clothe themselves with flocks, the valleys deck themselves with grain" (vv. 11–13).
- Psalm 90 is a prayer for help that meditates on the shortness of human life and asks God to grant wisdom, favor, joy, and prosperity.

As an example of a creation psalm, we will consider Psalm 8:

> [1] O LORD, our Sovereign,
>     how majestic is your name in all the earth!
>
> You have set your glory above the heavens.
>     [2] Out of the mouths of babes and infants

15. Other psalms are often included as creation psalms, including Pss. 33; 46; 144. Creation psalms also occur outside the Psalter, especially in Isa. 40–55 and the book of Job. In particular, see Amos 4:13; 5:8–9; and Hab. 3.

you have founded a bulwark because of your foes,
  to silence the enemy and the avenger.

[3] When I look at your heavens, the work of your fingers,
  the moon and the stars that you have established;
[4] what are human beings that you are mindful of them,
  mortals that you care for them?

[5] Yet you have made them a little lower than God,
  and crowned them with glory and honor.
[6] You have given them dominion over the works of your hands;
  you have put all things under their feet,
[7] all sheep and oxen,
  and also the beasts of the field,
[8] the birds of the air, and the fish of the sea,
  whatever passes along the paths of the seas.

[9] O Lord, our Sovereign,
  how majestic is your name in all the earth!

The poem begins and ends with the repetition of an identical phrase: "O Lord, our Sovereign, how majestic is your name in all the earth!" This poetic device is called an "inclusio" (see sidebar below). In the very middle of the psalm is a question: "What are human beings that you are mindful of them, mortals that you care for them?" This question centers the psalm, both thematically and spatially. In between the bookends, and around the center, the psalm explores the complex creation that the Lord has fashioned—from the grandly cosmic "moon" and "stars" right down to the earthily domestic "sheep and oxen." The question that the psalmist has is profound: In the midst of this

---

### ENDING THE WAY ONE STARTS

When a poem begins and ends identically, this is called an "inclusio." This is a poetic "bookending" technique, which accomplishes a couple of things artistically. An inclusio brings the poem to an elegant ending: it creates the sense of a good finish. The repetition of an inclusio also functions to fill out or round out the main theme of a poem, because the repetition of a phrase will sound a little different the final time it is read. In Psalm 8, for example, the first time the audience hears the phrase "how majestic is your name in all the earth," the emphasis is on the first half of the phrase: *how majestic is your name.* . . . But at the end of the poem, after all the talk in the psalm about the earth and nature and creation, the latter part of the sentence is stressed: . . . *in all the earth.*

vast creation, why would we imagine that God cares about little old us? The psalm's answer is right out of the "order" of creation. God cares about us because God has given us a special role to play in creation. Human beings are to be the stewards, the caretakers, of God's beloved creation. God has given human beings the responsibility for creation: God has placed all of creation "under their feet." Unpacking the poetry of the psalm, John Goldingay sums up its meaning this way:

> If we look one way, at the extraordinary nature of the cosmos as a whole, we can be overwhelmed by our insignificance. God bids us look the other way, at the earthly creation project that God still intends to complete, and in which we have a significant role. Our vocation is to work for the completing of God's creation project. . . . We can give ourselves to this implausible project, knowing that we are working with the grain of God's creation purpose.[16]

## "Those Who Do Not Learn from the Past Are Doomed to Repeat It"—Historical Psalms

Just for fun, think about something that went *really wrong* or *really right* in the last few years—something that people should know about, should learn from, should never, ever, ever, ever forget. Now, make a song out of it.

Don't have time? If you actually did take the time to write a song about something that happened in the past, it might be at least a little bit like the historical psalms.

The "historical" psalms are psalms that sing about the past in order to shape the future. As Richard Clifford has written, "'Historical' is put in quotation marks because these psalms tell the story of God's mighty acts rather than write history in a modern sense. Such narratives include Psalms 78, 105–6, 135–36."[17] The historical psalms each retell a portion of God's dealings with the people of Israel. As we have noticed above with the cases of royal psalms and creation psalms, in terms of form these psalms take the shape of one of the formal genres of psalms, and in terms of theme they expand on one or more aspects of Israel's sacred history.

- Psalm 78 is an instructional psalm in terms of form; in terms of history it relates parts of the story from the time of the exodus, through the wilderness wanderings, down to the time of King David.

16. John Goldingay, *Psalms 1–41*, vol. 1 of *Psalms* (Grand Rapids: Baker Academic, 2006), 161.
17. Richard J. Clifford, *Psalms 1–72* (Nashville: Abingdon, 2002), 23. The authors of this book also include Pss. 77; 89; and 132 among the historical psalms.

- Psalm 89 is a prayer for help in terms of form; in terms of history, it tells the story of God's choice of the house of David to produce the kings of Israel (vv. 19–37).

- Psalms 105 and 106 are praise psalms in terms of form (they begin and end with the typical call to praise: "Praise the LORD!"). Psalm 105 takes a positive view of Israel's history, focusing mainly on God's mighty deeds on Israel's behalf. Psalm 106, by contrast, takes a negative view, focusing on the history of Israel's repeated rebellions against God and failures to be faithful to God.

- Psalms 135–136 are hymns of praise that focus especially on God's rescue of Israel from slavery in Egypt and the gift of the promised land.

In order to get a sense of how to read the historical psalms, let us consider contrasting sections from two very similar psalms, 105 and 106. In each of the following passages, the psalms are describing Israel's slavery in Egypt and God's rescue of Israel:

### Psalm 105:23–26

Then Israel came to Egypt;
    Jacob lived as an alien in the land of Ham.
And the LORD made his people very fruitful,
    and made them stronger than their foes,
whose hearts he then turned to hate his people,
    to deal craftily with his servants.

He sent his servant Moses,
    and Aaron whom he had chosen.

### Psalm 106:7–10

Our ancestors, when they were in Egypt,
    did not consider your wonderful works;
they did not remember the abundance of your steadfast love,
    but rebelled against the Most High at the Red Sea.
Yet he saved them for his name's sake,
    so that he might make known his mighty power.
He rebuked the Red Sea, and it became dry;
    he led them through the deep as through a desert.
So he saved them from the hand of the foe,
    and delivered them from the hand of the enemy.

The two psalms—105 and 106—can be called twin psalms. They are very similar in form, length, style, and content. And they stand right next to each other in the book of Psalms. But if they are twins, they are fraternal twins rather than identical twins! If told, "There is both good news and bad news; which do you want to hear first?" the authors of Psalms 105 and 106 would make different choices. The first twin, Psalm 105, is a good-news-first kind of a storyteller. The story told in Psalm 105 focuses on the good news of God's mighty deeds on Israel's behalf. The storyteller wants the community to know what a powerful and faithful God it has. The second twin, Psalm 106, is a bad-news-first kind of a storyteller. The story is still good news! But the storyteller in Psalm 106 wants the community to know that it is very prone to sin; the psalmist wants the community to recognize how much it is prone to violence and hurting one another. And once the community knows this, Psalm 106 wants the community to recognize how forgiving and loving its God is.

The point of the historical psalms is not to learn the dates and names and events of Israel's history. Rather, the point of the historical psalms is *to learn from* the dates and names and events of Israel's history.

In order to read the historical psalms, the reader needs to ask, *What claim does the story that is being told make on me or us?* Is the story making a claim about who I am? Is the story making a claim about how I should act? Is the story making a claim that is a promise to me?

## Other Thematically Defined Psalms

There are several other types of psalms that are defined by their similar thematic content. We will close this chapter by briefly describing each of these types of psalms.

### Penitential Psalms

The term "penitential psalm" refers to a subgroup of the prayers for help (also called lament psalms). The penitential psalms all share a common theme: the pray-er asks for forgiveness from sins. These prayers for help are prayed by a person who was caught in a mess of their own making. They broke some law, hurt some person, or committed some crime. Now they are praying and asking to be delivered from the bed they have made for themselves. Traditionally, in Western Christianity, seven psalms have been labeled as penitential psalms: 6; 32; 38; 51; 102; 130; and 143. Psalm 51 is the model penitential psalm. As the superscription of the psalm says, it is traditionally associated with the time in King David's life "when the prophet Nathan came to him, after he had gone in to Bathsheba." That story, which can be found in 2 Samuel 11–12, tells of how a prophet confronted David after he impregnated Uriah's wife and then killed Uriah to cover up the sin. Psalm 51 offers words of repentance for such a time:

> Have mercy on me, O God,
>     according to your steadfast love;
> according to your abundant mercy
>     blot out my transgressions.
> Wash me thoroughly from my iniquity,
>     and cleanse me from my sin.
>
> For I know my transgressions,
>     and my sin is ever before me. (vv. 1–3)

Strangely, there are some other psalms in which the psalmist prays for forgiveness (for example, Ps. 25:11 reads, "For your name's sake, O Lord, pardon my guilt, for it is great"). Even more strangely, some of these psalms called penitential, such as Psalm 6, do not explicitly mention sin or forgiveness.

Although these psalms do not contain any words of forgiveness, they nevertheless bear witness to one of Israel's central confessions about humans and about God—that humans sin against each other and against God, but that the Lord is a forgiving God. As one of the penitential psalms says, "If you, Lord, kept a record of sins, Lord, who could stand? But with you there is forgiveness, so that we can, with reverence, serve you" (130:3–4 NIV).

### Imprecatory Psalms

The so-called imprecatory psalms are somewhat the reverse image of the penitential psalms. Both are subtypes of the prayer for help. But whereas in penitential psalms the supplicant prays for deliverance from oneself and from personal sins, in the imprecatory psalms, the pray-er asks for deliverance from one's enemies:

> Let them be put to shame and dishonor
>     who seek after my life.
> Let them be turned back and confounded
>     who devise evil against me.
> Let them be like chaff before the wind,
>     with the angel of the Lord driving them on.
> Let their way be dark and slippery,
>     with the angel of the Lord pursuing them.
>
> For without cause they hid their net for me;
>     without cause they dug a pit for my life. (35:4–7)

Other imprecatory poems include Psalms 69; 83; 88; 109; 137; 139 (vv. 19–22); and 140. These psalms often disturb modern people of faith, who wonder, "What are these prayers doing in the Bible? Why are God's people asking for others to be harmed?" These prayers are especially troubling to some Christians who have been influenced by Christ to "turn the other [cheek]" and to "love your enemies and pray for those who persecute you" (Matt. 5:39, 44).

In understanding these poems, four things should be kept in mind. First, these poems are utterly human. They give voice to genuine human emotions. Faith does not ignore or completely suppress such emotions. There is honesty here. Second, although these prayers give voice to human emotions, pray-ers do not take violence into their own hands. Romans 12:19 says that vengeance belongs to God, meaning that humans should not take matters of justice into their own hands but instead leave paybacks to God. By praying these psalms, the psalmists give their anger away to God: they name the injustice that they are feeling, then hand over the matter of vengeance to God. Third, those of us who live in basically orderly societies can forget how chaotic most societies have been during most periods of history. For those who prayed these psalms, as well as for many people alive today, the only "deliverance from evil" that people can imagine is for the evildoers to be eliminated: the only possible rescue from oppression is the removal of the oppressors. Fourth, and finally, we should remember that someone out there might be praying this prayer

## PLANES, TRAINS, AND AUTOMOBILES

Like the songs of ancient Israel, American songs can be grouped in different ways. For example, there is rock 'n' roll, country western, hip-hop and rap, and jazz.

But American songs can also be grouped according to common themes. There are love songs, of course. And brokenhearted songs. And in country music, there are a lot of songs about trains. But our favorite group of thematically related songs are "car songs." Just think about all the great car songs in American music: "Hot Rod Lincoln" and "Mercury Blues," "Little Deuce Coupe" and "Little Red Corvette," "Brand New Cadillac" and "Cadillac Ranch," "Highway Patrol" and "State Trooper," "Silver Thunderbird" and "Pink Cadillac."

Imagine that you are a historian who lives two thousand years in the future, and the automobile no longer exists. What could you learn about life in twenty-first-century America by studying all of the car songs? You might learn that cars are a symbol of freedom and independence but also of danger and death.

In a similar way, scholars today can learn a great deal about ancient Israel by studying the various psalms about the king, or Jerusalem, or history, and so on.

against *us*. These psalms ask us to reflect not just on God's justice but also on our own participation in injustice. Have we participated in oppression in such a way that somewhere out there someone is praying about us, "Let them be put to shame and dishonor" (35:4)?

### Zion Psalms

Zion psalms are a subgroup of the hymns of praise. These psalms celebrate Zion—a name for the mount in Jerusalem on which the temple was built, and therefore also a name for Jerusalem itself—as the place in which God has chosen to dwell. The psalms often celebrate God's promises, such as the promise God made to David that one or another of his descendants would forever be king of God's people (89:35–37) or the promise that God made to Abraham that his descendants would be blessed to be a blessing (105:9–10). The Zion psalms celebrate God's promise that God will be with the chosen people in Jerusalem, loving them and protecting them from evil. Psalm 46, the psalm on which Martin Luther based the famous hymn "A Mighty Fortress Is Our God," is probably the most well-known Zion psalm:

> There is a river whose streams make glad the city of God,
> > the holy habitation of the Most High.
> God is in the midst of the city; it shall not be moved;
> > God will help it when the morning dawns.
> The nations are in an uproar, the kingdoms totter;
> > he utters his voice, the earth melts.
> The LORD of hosts is with us;
> > the God of Jacob is our refuge. (vv. 4–7)

These psalms often seem strange to modern people, in part because modern technology and transportation have made us so mobile and rendered "distance" an almost meaningless concept. Most of us no longer have any permanent attachment to any particular place. This is especially true of Protestant Christians, who have such an elevated sense of "the Word" that they are even more disconnected from the idea of a holy place. Roman Catholics, with their connection to Rome and the Vatican, and Jews, with their connection to the Holy Land, have more of a sense of holy place than Protestants do.

Perhaps the best way for a modern to understand what Jerusalem meant to the ancient Israelites is to liken the role that Jerusalem played for them to the role that the Bible or Holy Communion plays for some modern Christians. Similar to the holy words of the Bible or the holy body and blood of the Lord's Supper, many ancient Israelites looked on the city—its walls, its temple, its strength—as a "means of grace." Thus, they could look at the city and say, "Walk about Zion, go all around it, count its towers. . . . Tell the next generation that this is God, our God forever and ever" (48:12, 13b–14).

### Liturgical Psalms

A final group is often identified as the liturgical psalms. These psalms give indication of having been used in some liturgical fashion, either in the temple in Jerusalem or in a later synagogue or village setting. As one can guess, it is hard to make a decisive judgment about which psalms suggest evidence of a liturgical setting. Some psalms seem to indicate a setting in worship liturgy. Psalm 15, for example, begins with what appears to be the question of a person about to enter the temple. And the rest of the psalm appears to be a liturgical answer to the question.

> O Lord, who may abide in your tent?
>   Who may dwell on your holy hill?
>
> Those who walk blamelessly, and do what is right,
>     and speak the truth from their heart;
>   who do not slander with their tongue,
>     and do no evil to their friends,
>       nor take up a reproach against their neighbors. (vv. 1–3)

---

### GOD IS WITH "HER"

There is a television series, based on a comic book story, called *Warrior Nun*. The series is about a paraplegic orphan girl, Ava (played by Alba Baptista), who dies and is miraculously animated (possessed?) by an ancient artifact in the form of an angelic halo that is pressed into her back. Brought back to life, she is able to walk and far more. In a voiceover she asks, "What are you up to, God?" Each episode of the limited series is titled by a chapter and verse from the Bible, which is meant to shape one's understanding of the chapter of the story that is about to unfold. The very first episode is titled "Psalm 46:5," which reads,

> God is in the midst of her; she shall not be moved;
>   God will help her as the morning dawns. (AT)

What is interesting about this is that the "she" in the psalm actually refers to the "city of God" (see v. 4). Plucked out of context, however, the psalm claims God's care, provision, and power for the titular character, saying that the "Lord of hosts" is with "her" (cf. 46:7, 11).

Other psalms have small indications of liturgical action but do not seem to be a full liturgy. Psalm 47, for example, starts out with "Clap your hands, all you people." If one defines a liturgical psalm as a composition intended for worship and in which more than one voice speaks, the following psalms may be tentatively identified as liturgies: 15; 24; 29; 91; 95; 115; 118; 121; 134; and 136. In addition, four psalms seem to have been composed to play a role in one or more of Israel's major annual "festivals" (Passover, Weeks, and Booths): 50; 74; 81; and 95. These psalms may be studied in order to help us gather some sense of what happened in Israel's worship life and also to develop a sense of what central beliefs informed Israel's worship. But based only on these texts, it is impossible to reconstruct what a typical worship service might have looked like in ancient Israel.

## Conclusion

This chapter expanded on the concept of genre—a concept that was initially introduced in the previous chapter. Knowing the genre of a piece of writing is critical to understanding it because the context in which words occur contributes to what those words mean. The previous chapter argued that the Psalter contains two types of genres: those classified according to their common "forms" and those classified according to common "themes" or "content." The second of these types of genre—genre that share common themes and content—was the focus of this chapter. Specifically, this chapter introduced (1) royal psalms (which are about the human king), (2) enthronement psalms (which proclaim the Lord is king), (3) wisdom or instructional psalms (which seek to teach the reader), (4) creation psalms (which describe nature as the creation of a loving God), and (5) historical psalms (which describe God's activity in history, especially on behalf of Israel).

―――――――――――――― **GOING DEEPER** ――――――――――――――

In order to deepen your grasp of the concepts introduced in this chapter, consider doing one or more of the following exercises:

1. The royal psalms and Zion psalms pay tribute to Israel's belief that the institutions of the Davidic kings and the city of Jerusalem were agents through which God worked (in spite of the imperfections of both institutions). Think of a political or social institution that you

value—such as the executive or judicial arms of the United States government, or a charitable organization such as the United Way, or a local institution such as the school system—and write a psalm in praise of that institution.

2. The wisdom or instructional psalms take a teaching tone, offering instruction to future generations of young people. Think of some basic life lessons that you wished you had known when you were ten years old, then write a letter or poem to yourself at that age.

3. The imprecatory psalms give voice to the anger of people who were suffering at the hands of oppressors. Think of someone you are really angry with at the moment or whom you were angry with at some time in the past. Abraham Lincoln is said to have written letters to people he was very angry with. Then he would seal the letter and *not send it*. Write a letter either to God or to a person you are angry with. In the letter, pour out all of your anger. *Then burn or shred that letter: do not send it!*

## FOR FURTHER READING

Brueggemann, Walter. *The Psalms and the Life of Faith*. Minneapolis: Fortress, 1995.

DeClaissé-Walford, Nancy. *Introduction to the Psalms*. St. Louis: Chalice, 2004.

McCann, J. Clinton. *A Theological Introduction to the Book of Psalms*. Nashville: Abingdon, 1993.

Miller, Patrick D. *Interpreting the Psalms*. Philadelphia: Fortress, 1986.

# FOUR

# What Is a Psalmist?

*Learning to Understand the Voice*
*and Life Situations of the Psalms*

### Introducing the Concept of Voice and Place

If you are a psalmist, does that mean that you do psalmy things? Or that you are a little bit psalmish? Granted, these are silly questions, but what is a psalmist anyway? "Psalmist" is a term used generically to talk about the author of a psalm or of a collection of psalms. This is similar to the way one might talk about the voice of a song as "the singer" or the voice of a poem as "the poet."

When people read a poem or listen to a song, they tend to imagine or "supply" a speaker for the poem or song. This is especially true when a poem or song is sung from a first-person point of view, using terms such as "I," "my," "me," "we," "our," and "us."[1] Readers or listeners may not even be aware that they are imagining who the speaker of a poem is, but doing so is often necessary in order to understand a poem. If a song is sung from a first-person-singular perspective, the listener needs to imagine who the "I"

---

1. There is an explicit "I" in about 65 percent of the psalms (98 out of 150). There is an explicit "we" or "our" in around 30 percent of the psalms (46 out of 150). The extent to which the individual "I" or "we" is present in any given psalm depends, as might be expected, on the given psalm.

is that sings the song. Based on various clues and hints within the song, the listener builds up an imagined picture of the singer. And then in turn, based on that imagined picture, the listener makes sense of the rest of the words of the song. For example, consider the first two stanzas of an old folk song titled "The Water Is Wide."

> The water is wide, I can't cross over,
> And neither have I wings to fly.
> Build me a boat that can carry two,
> And both shall row, my love and I.
>
> There is a ship and she sails the sea,
> She's loaded deep, as deep can be.
> But not as deep as the love I'm in,
> I know not how, to sink or swim.

The song is sung from the perspective of "I." As you read the lyrics to the song, how do you imagine the "I" of the song? Do you imagine a male or female? How old? Where is the singer standing? What is the singer looking at? What are the singer's emotions? What has motivated the singer to utter this song?

There are a range of possible answers to these questions—many of which may be legitimate. The voice could be male or female. It may be older or younger. You may imagine the singer literally standing on the shore of a sea . . . or not. The person may be deeply sad or merely wistful and nostalgic.

But there are also some unlikely ways (or even unhelpful ways) to imagine the voice of the song. Thus, it is unlikely that the singer is a hippopotamus. It is unlikely that we would imagine the singer as being motivated by an intense desire to win a game. It is also unlikely that the "I" of the song is a three-year-old human being. In truth, a three-year-old could memorize the words of the song and sing it. But even if you heard a three-year-old sing the song, you probably would still imagine an adult human as the voice of the song.

When people read a psalm, most of which are written from a first-person perspective, they imagine some person or persons as the voice(s) speaking the psalm. The "psalmist" is the generic term that scholars use to speak about the supplied voice that utters the psalms.

The reason why scholars have come to refer generically to the author of a given psalm as "the psalmist" is because most of the psalms are anonymous compositions: we do not know who wrote them. Yet *somebody* wrote them. There must have been some flesh-and-blood human being who first spoke the words of a psalm, or first set reed or pen to parchment or papyrus, or someone who first commissioned the writing of a given psalm. Consider the following example:

Psalm 2 simply begins,

> Why do the nations conspire,
>> and the peoples plot in vain?

In verse 7 we encounter the "I," the one who is singing the psalm:

> I will tell of the decree of the LORD:
> He said to me, "You are my son;
>> today I have begotten you."

At this point, a reader of the psalm may wonder, "Who is this 'I' that is now speaking?" In the context of the psalm itself, it seems clear that the one who is speaking, the "I," is the Judean king. Further, searching the rest of the psalm, the reader can learn that the "I" is one who is identified as "anointed" by God (v. 2), the king on Zion (the name of the hill in Jerusalem on which the temple once stood), one who is promised rulership over "the nations" of the world (v. 8). So, although the psalmist is not explicitly named, the psalm is placed upon the lips of the king, who in Psalm 2 plays the part of the psalmist.

Does this mean that we should understand all of the psalms as being spoken by the Judean king? No. It is clear from the first verse of Psalm 72, for example, that it is spoken by one other than the king: "Give the king your justice, O God, and your righteousness to a king's son." Therefore, when coming to each individual psalm, the reader needs to imagine who the psalmist of *this* psalm is.

Another example is Psalm 104. Like Psalm 2, the psalm jumps right in without any indication about who is speaking. But unlike Psalm 2, there is less clear information that might help a reader draw a clear conclusion about who the "I" might be. Psalm 104 begins,

> Bless the Lord, O my soul.
> O LORD my God, you are very great.

There is clearly a psalmist at work, who addresses himself or herself as "my soul," but we hear about this psalmist only at the beginning of the psalm and then at the very end of the poem:

> I will sing to the LORD as long as I live;
>> I will sing praise to my God while I have being.

> May my meditation be pleasing to him,
> for I rejoice in the LORD.
> Let sinners be consumed from the earth,
> And let the wicked be no more.
> Bless the LORD, O my soul.
> Praise the LORD! (vv. 33–35)

There are not many clues in this psalm that would allow much clarity about who this "I" is, other than that the "I" is a psalmist. But in the last couple of verses, the text does offer some clues about what the author's motivation may have been for writing the psalm: it is a meditation on the glory of the creator-God. Because the "I" is a singer—"I will sing to the LORD"—we can guess that perhaps the psalmist may have been a temple musician or a priest whose duties included leading temple worship. But this conclusion is not foolproof, because elsewhere in the Old Testament, people other than temple musicians can be heard singing to God. For example, Moses and his sister Miriam both sang praise to the Lord at the edge of the Red Sea (Exod. 15). Deborah and Barak sang after a military victory (Judg. 5). Hannah sang a song after she dedicated her son to serve the Lord (1 Sam. 2). King David sang a song of lament after the death of his friend Jonathan (2 Sam. 1) and a song of praise after victory in battle (2 Sam. 22). The prophet Amos sang a song of mourning as a way of criticizing the immoral character of the people of Israel (Amos 5). And so on. Therefore, we must be cautious even about a very general designation such as assigning the psalmist of Psalm 104 a vague identity such as "a temple singer." Even if Psalm 104 was authored by a temple singer, the song's performance may not have been limited to being sung in the temple during a formal worship service.

All of which is to say that the act of imagining the "I" of a psalm, what one imagines about the identity of the psalmist, is a *necessary* part of trying to understand a psalm, but it is a part of interpretation that one must hold loosely. As you read a psalm, go ahead and try to imagine who the ancient "voice" of the psalm was. But do not get too fixated either on getting it exactly right or insisting that your particular view is the only (or even the best) way to imagine who the psalmist was. Rather, in the words of the poem "Introduction to Poetry" that was quoted in the introduction to this book, imagine who the psalmist was so that you can "walk inside" the poet's room, or "waterski across the surface of a poem waving at the author's name on the shore," or "press an ear against its hive."[2]

---

2. Billy Collins, *The Apple That Astonished Paris: Poems* (Fayetteville: University of Arkansas Press, 1988), 58.

## Excursus: Understanding the Psalm Superscriptions

In chapter 1, the reader was introduced to the term "superscription," which refers to words that occur at the start of a psalm, before the psalm itself begins. In most English translations of the psalms, as in this book, these superscriptions are not labeled with a verse number.

Some readers interpret some of the superscriptions as identifying the authors of some of the psalms. Seventy-four different psalms, for example, include the words "of David" somewhere in the superscription. Many people have taken these words to mean that King David wrote these psalms. For this reason, in the Muslim Qur'an, the Psalms themselves are referred to as "David." It is also why Peter (see Acts 4:25–26, which quotes Ps. 2:7) and the author of Hebrews (see Heb. 4:7, which quotes Ps. 95:7–8) attribute to David psalms that do not include the words "of David" in their respective superscriptions.

In addition to a psalm "of Moses" (Ps. 90), there is one "of Heman" (88) and another "of Ethan" (89), both of whom are referred to as Ezrahites. There are two psalms "of Solomon" (72; 127). There is a collection associated with an individual, Asaph (50; 73–83). And another collection is associated with a group, the "sons of Korah" (often translated as "Korahites"; 42; 44–49; 84–85; 87–88).

Scholars disagree about what the phrases such as "of David" or "of Moses" or "of the sons of Korah" mean. The Hebrew words themselves literally mean "to David" and "to Moses" and "to the sons of Korah." Those who take the phrase to indicate who the authors of the psalms were interpret this word "to" as a shorthand phrase for "belonging to David" or "belonging to Moses."

But there are several other possibilities. It is not always clear exactly what "to David/Asaph/Solomon" is intended to mean. The phrase may indicate a dedication to a particular person, such as "dedicated to David." It could indicate artistic inspiration: "inspired by David." Or it may have indicated authorship: "written by David." The phrase might also indicate to which collection of psalms a particular psalm belongs: "belonging to the David collection." It might indicate the location where a particular group of psalms was collected: "part of the city of David collection." One thing that is clear is that the 150 psalms of the Psalter are a collection of smaller collections. Most likely these smaller collections of psalms existed independently before they were incorporated into the Psalter. In this way of thinking, the psalms "of David" belonged to a collection of psalms that were kept in the royal temple of the Davidic kings, the psalms "of the sons of Korah" were originally collected somewhere else, and the "songs of ascents" (Pss. 120–134) were collected in yet a third setting, and so on.

The authors of this book do not believe that the phrases "of David" or "of Asaph" originally were meant to indicate authorship.[3] What does seem clear, however, is that *at some point in time* the interpretation of the phrases "of David" or "of

---

3. A primary reason for this conclusion is that many of the psalms "of David" refer to the temple in Jerusalem, which was not built until after David's death.

Asaph" evolved to the point where they were taken by many to be an attribution of authorship. In our approach, we do not take these phrases to indicate who the authors of the psalms were; rather, we think of them as anonymous compositions. But the superscriptions are still important since they often tell us how the psalms were interpreted or used very early in the tradition. In this way we think of the superscriptions as evidence of the very earliest interpretation of these poems. And in that way they are very helpful for reading the psalms.

Not every psalm has a superscription, and not every psalm superscription is about a person or persons. Some of the psalms have superscriptions that shape how readers might understand the persona or voice of a psalm. Psalm 92 bears this superscription: "A Psalm. A Song for the Sabbath Day." The superscription indicates that the psalm was used for Sabbath-day worship. It probably does not mean the psalm was composed for the Sabbath but rather that at some point the poem was adopted for that purpose, presumably for the use by any Sabbath worshiper, but again there is a discernible "I" in the psalm: "It is good to give thanks to the LORD. . . . You have exalted my horn like that of the wild ox; you have poured over me fresh oil" (vv. 1a, 10). Presumably the "I" in this psalm stands for any Sabbath worshiper, during any age or epoch. Similarly, Psalm 30's superscription includes the words "A Psalm. A Song at the dedication of the temple. Of David." The Hebrew word for "dedication" is ḥanukkah. Although the psalm probably was not originally written for the Jewish celebration of Hanukkah—which commemorates the rededication of the temple in 164 BCE, during the Maccabean period—over time the psalm came to be read at that festival. Read in that context, the persona or "I" of the psalm—"I will extol you, O LORD, for you have drawn me up" (30:1)—stands for any worshiper at Hanukkah. A final example of how the superscriptions shape readers' understanding of the persona of a psalm is the superscription of Psalm 102: "A prayer of one afflicted, when faint and pleading before the LORD." This superscription indicates that anyone who is suffering is invited to pray Psalm 102 on one's own behalf. It is an invitation for each reader to become, at least for the duration of how long it takes to utter the psalm, the "I" who cries to God. The psalm then begins with a cry to God for help:

> HEAR MY PRAYER, O LORD;
> let my cry come to you.

Whose prayer is this? Who is behind this "my"? The psalm does not say: it is simply "of one afflicted," so presumably any such person can pray this psalm. The "psalmist" is simply anyone who has experienced affliction, who is feeling alone and attacked on all fronts. The identity of the original author of the psalm and the situation of that psalmist are unclear. Yet this ambiguity is helpful because it means that any person in any situation of suffering can pray the psalm. It is available to all.

## The Role of Persona in the Psalms

To pursue the question of "Who is the psalmist?" is to engage a combination of two interpretive realities that invite the reader into the interpretive and experiential world of the psalm. These two realities are *the voice of the pray-er* and *the situation in which the pray-er finds oneself praying*. Or to put it another way, the author of the psalm stages the poem in such a way that a particular voice is heard or experienced. The pray-er of the psalm then takes up this anthem, borrowing language that is in harmony with the current personal situation, and in so doing seeks to make sense of one's own world. To ask who the psalmist is, and to think about the relationship that the reader may have with this "person" who composed the poem, leads to asking the basic but important question of who the persona is in the psalm and what that persona means to me.

When reading poetry, it is helpful to think about the voice of the poem as "the persona" rather than as "the narrator," as we tend to think of the voice that tells a story. The idea of persona in the psalms is helpful because poetry creates meaning differently than does prose or storytelling.

When reading a story, understanding of meaning usually takes place as one seeks to understand the characters, place, and developing plot of that story. The narrator tells the tale, and the listener/reader responds to that story, identifying with one character, person, situation, or element of the narrative more than another character. For instance, when reading the Harry Potter stories, a female may identify more with Hermione, while a male may identify more with Harry. Or again, an older person may identify more with Dumbledore, while a younger person may identify more with Ginny.

In poetry—particularly the poetry of prayer, praise, and thanksgiving— understanding of meaning happens more in the moment as a reader experiences the emotions and expressions of the poem. In this sense, a reader becomes part of the experience of the poem in a much more direct manner: by identifying oneself with the voice speaking the poem (one imagines oneself either as the speaker of the poem or as the audience to which the voice of the poem is speaking).

In the psalms this is accomplished in large part through the emotional and imaginative exchange between the psalmist and the psalm reader, psalm pray-er, or psalm singer. The experience of the psalmist, the "I" of the poem, becomes the vehicle of experience or expression of the psalm reader. This can happen in different ways. For example, a reader can imagine him- or herself as the "I" or the speaker of the poem: the reader can "put on" the identity of the poem's persona. To use another example, the reader can imagine oneself as "overhearing" the voice of the psalmist: the reader can try to empathize with the speaker's situation and emotions. Or again, the reader can imagine oneself as the audience to whom the psalmist is speaking: here one "puts on" the identity of the psalmist's audience. In each of these examples, we can imagine that poetry creates meaning more directly than a story creates meaning, because the voice of the psalm speaks either directly *to the reader* or speaks *for the reader*.

By way of example, read the following excerpts from Psalm 18. As you do so, imagine who the "I" (the persona) of the psalm might be:

> I love you, O LORD, my strength.
> The LORD is my rock, my fortress, and my deliverer,
>    my God, my rock in whom I take refuge,
>    my shield, and the horn of my salvation, my stronghold.
> I call upon the LORD, who is worthy to be praised,
>    so I shall be saved from my enemies.
>
> . . . . . . . . . . . . . . . . . . . . . . . . . . . . . . . . . . . . . . . .
>
> In my distress I called upon the LORD;
>    to my God I cried for help.
>
> . . . . . . . . . . . . . . . . . . . . . . . . . . . . . . . . . . . . . . . .
>
> For I have kept the ways of the LORD,
>    and have not wickedly departed from my God.
> For all his ordinances were before me,
>    and his statutes I did not put away from me.
> I was blameless before him,
>    and I kept myself from guilt. (vv. 1–3, 6a, 21–23)[4]

This "I" is the persona of the psalm: the one who is praying, calling for help, confessing sin, praising God. After identifying what is at stake for the persona presented by the psalmist, the reader of the psalm can understand issues, evaluate those challenges, and apply them to one's own life. Based only on the verses that were quoted above, it would be hard to identify the speaker as anything more than an individual who went through a crisis. Based on other parts of the psalm and based on special language that occurs in the poem, Psalm 18 is usually considered to be a royal song of thanksgiving. That is, it is a psalm that was sung after deliverance from a time of crisis; and it is a royal psalm in which the "I" is assumed to be the king.

---

4. There are many other "I/me/my" statements in Ps. 18 as well, in vv. 28–29, 33–40, 42–44, 47–49.

Read again the parts of the psalm that were quoted above. How does your understanding of the psalm change if you imagine the psalm as spoken by a Judean king (instead of however you imagined the speaker when you first read the verses)?

"Persona" is the aspect of someone's character or person that is perceivable by others. In literary terms "persona" is usually a way of thinking about the person or character being presented. For example, this might be the public face of a celebrity as presented by a public relations agency, or the "mask" that the actor presents of a character onstage—in some ways this is a fictive face, or at least a presented face that is not intended as a whole picture of who the actor truly is. Persona, then, is what is presented, the face that is put on by a performer who presents the poem.

When we read a psalm, a host of possible figures are involved: the author of the psalm, the voice of the imagined speaker of the psalm, the community for which it is written or to whom it is imagined as spoken, the figure presented within the psalm, and the reader of the psalm. But the "I" is in many ways the *most important* because it allows the reader of the psalm to assume the persona of the psalmist. Because poetry brings to life an immediate reexperiencing of emotion, of shared feeling about a situation or need, the reader of the psalm may take up the words of the psalmist, putting on the life setting, adopting it as one's own. In this sense persona is a vital point of entry into understanding and interpreting a psalm because it establishes and allows for a sense of likeness between psalmist and psalm reader. The persona presented in the psalm is "like" my own face; the psalm offers a like circumstance, with similar words to speak in and to it.

## The Idea of Life Situation in the Psalms

It has been widely observed that one finds in the psalms both the highs and the lows of life, and much that comes in between. The psalms resonate with the highs and lows of daily life. The psalms are very much the heart—felt and expressed—of biblical faith and religion. As Sigmund Mowinckel put it, "In the psalms the human heart has found its counterpart at all times, in sorrow and in happiness, as an individual and as a member of God's People."[5] This is true in large part because the life situations represented via the persona of the psalmist are readily understandable and applicable by the careful reader.

5. Sigmund Mowinckel, *The Psalms in Israel's Worship*, 2 vols. (Nashville: Abingdon, 1962), 1:1.

Life situation (our way of talking about the idea of the "setting in life" or "life setting") has to do with the imagined situation out of which a psalm arose and into which the reader of that psalm is invited. Let us return to the example of the old folk song "The Water Is Wide."

Earlier we asked you to imagine who the "I" of the song might be. Now imagine the "what" and the "when" and the "why" of the song.

> The water is wide, I can't cross over,
> And neither have I wings to fly.
> Build me a boat that can carry two,
> And both shall row, my love and I.
>
> There is a ship and she sails the sea,
> She's loaded deep, as deep can be.
> But not as deep as the love I'm in,
> I know not how, to sink or swim.

Where do you imagine the singer standing? What body of water do you imagine? Why is the singer moved to give voice to these words? Picture two different possible scenarios. First, imagine the singer as a young, male American pioneer who has crossed the wide Missouri River and is now separated for a time from his lover by the river's waters.

Second, imagine the singer as a middle-aged Irish mother whose son has sailed to America to start a new life, and she is permanently separated from him: she will never see her child again. This rings in one's ears slightly differently based on how one imagines the "what" and the "when" and the "why" of the song. This "why, where, and when" of how a reader imagines a psalm being spoken or sung is called the life situation of the psalm.

The life situations of the psalms run a full range of circumstances, from times of celebration and joy, to family matters, to personal struggles with depression, to national times of trial, to the feeling of being attacked or slandered by other people.

Some life situations are explicitly tied to corporate times of worship as the community of God's people gathers in the sanctuary. We turn to those below. For now, we explore some examples of life situations that appear in the psalms and are primarily geared toward the individual.

When reading a psalm with an eye to understanding the life situation that it reflects, one effective place to start is to return to the persona represented in the psalm. When a psalm reveals its "I," showing its concern for "me" or "my," there is often some evidence of the setting out of which the psalm arises or, to put it another way, the reason the psalm is being written. Psalm

22 is an excellent example of this, with the psalmist complaining about his personal situation, which leads him to lament his suffering, even rejecting his own humanity:

> My God, my God, why have you forsaken me?
>     Why are you so far from helping me,
>         from the words of my groaning? (v. 1)

"My" situation, the perception that God is far from "me" and that "I" am surrounded by enemies on all sides who bite and tear at me, reveals a *situation of suffering and (perhaps) betrayal*. This harsh life situation prompts the "I am" cry of this particular psalmist in words that have had lasting power:

> But I am a worm, and not human;
>     scorned by others, and despised by the people. (v. 6)

The feeling of being less than human, of being marginalized and rejected, shapes both how the psalm itself is formed and how the reader of the psalm is then able to both understand and apply it.

Similar "I am" statements appear frequently in the psalms and are indicators of the struggles and joys that gave rise to these psalms. Reading with an eye to life situation requires imagination.

*"I am" in trouble or "I am" sick*. In Psalm 6:6–7 we can imagine the psalmist struggling through the long, lonely watches of the night:

> I *am weary* with my moaning;
>     every night I flood my bed with tears;
>     I drench my couch with my weeping.
> My eyes waste away because of grief;
>     they grow weak because of all my foes.

The initial situation in which the psalmist found himself was one of heart-wrenching sorrow, perhaps as a result of illness (see v. 2). The psalm then turns to refute the psalmist's enemies. They are rejected because God has heard the psalmist's prayer for help:

> Depart from me, all you workers of evil,
>     for the LORD has heard the sound of my weeping.
> The LORD has heard my supplication;
>     the LORD accepts my prayer.
> All my enemies shall be ashamed and struck with terror;
>     they shall turn back, and in a moment be put to shame. (vv. 8–10)

The overall life situation of the psalm can be imagined as one of conflict between a person who has been ill and his enemies, who seem to be exulting in his suffering, or claiming that his illness is deserved or his own fault, or even claiming that there is no help for the psalmist in God (cf. Ps. 3:2).

The setting of Psalm 39 is at once similar and different. There are enemies, "the wicked" (v. 1), before whom the psalmist is silent, but his silence is less about the wicked and more about his own wickedness:

> I am silent;
>> I do not open my mouth, for it is you who have done it.
> Remove your stroke from me;
>> I am worn down by the blows of your hand.
> You chastise mortals in punishment for sin,
>> consuming like a moth what is dear to them;
>> surely everyone is a mere breath. (vv. 9–11)

The psalmist feels keenly the results of sin. The "I" self-identifies as one who is experiencing punishment for sins he has committed, and he asks for forgiveness. Psalm 38 does something similar in identifying the psalmist's illness as a result of his sin: "My wounds grow foul and fester because of my foolishness" (v. 5). Other psalms do the same (Pss. 25; 51; 90). The life situations of these psalms, which may be discerned from the ways in which the psalmists describe their experiences, make it possible for the reader to try to come to grips with the content of a given psalm in context.

Thinking about the life situation of the psalm *requires imagination*. Two different readers will imagine the life situation of a given psalm in two different ways. The goal is not to be right but to read with imagination in order to make one's reading meaningful. Attention to life situation makes it possible to have a meaningful experience of reading, as a way of listening to what a poem says and then to interpret its meaning. As we will see, this is not always easy, but attention to the life situation is essential to a full and rich reading of a psalm.

There are two different aspects to the life situation of a psalm. One aspect has to do with what one might call the psalmist's physical and social situations: what was happening in the psalmist's life—be it physical, emotional, communal, or legal—that spurred the person to cry out to the Lord. Another aspect has to do with what one might call the psalmist's spiritual situation: what was happening in the psalmist's heart and mind and understanding of God that spurred the person to cry out to the Lord. Some psalms scholars have emphasized one of these alternatives to the exclusion of others. For example, Erhard Gerstenberger has tended to emphasize physical and social situations.

## "COVERING" THE PSALMS

One way to think about the persona of the psalms—or the "voice" of the psalms—is to think about musical artists who "cover" other artists' songs.

It is a common occurrence for musicians to take up a song that has been a hit by some other artist and to rerelease the song as a "cover." A few examples:

- Eric Clapton once covered "I Shot the Sheriff (But I Did Not Shoot the Deputy)," which was originally a hit for Bob Marley.
- Whitney Houston produced a great hit with her cover of Dolly Parton's song "I Will Always Love You."
- Johnny Cash, at the end of his life, covered the Nine Inch Nails song "Hurt."
- The band Wheezer covered the Toto song "Africa."

When the new artists covered these songs, they made them their own. They took the words and music that already existed, but by putting their own style and artistry to the songs, they claimed them as their own.

Dolly Parton originally wrote "I Will Always Love You" when she split from a musical partner and went on her own as a solo act. The song was a limited hit on country radio. When Whitney Houston released the song as part of the soundtrack of a romantic movie in which she starred, the song became a love song—and was a huge hit.

The Nine Inch Nails song "Hurt" originally conveyed a sense of meaningless-ness and nihilism. But when Johnny Cash, a devout Christian, covered the song at the end of his life, his voice sang the song as a gospel song. Cash changed the line "I wear this crown of sh—" to "I wear this crown of thorns"—an allusion to the story of Christ's crucifixion.

When modern readers pray or sing the psalms as their own, we can imagine them "covering" the psalms. The life situations from which they pray the psalms are to some extent different than those of the ancient authors. By singing and praying the psalms in new situations, they make the songs their own. The old, old psalms speak in a new, new way.

He wrote that the meaning of the psalms "have to be evaluated in their interrelation with life situations and social settings."[6] But Claus Westermann tended to emphasize the spiritual life situations of the psalmist. He wrote that "the observation that the life situation of the Psalms is the [earthly] cult cannot really be right. For that which really, in the last analysis, occurs in the

---

6. Erhard Gerstenberger, *Psalms, Part 1, with an Introduction to Cultic Poetry* (Grand Rapids: Eerdmans, 1988), 35.

Psalms is prayer."[7] So Westermann emphasized that the real context in which both praise is sung and prayers for help are prayed is the spiritual relationship between believers and God.

In the examples that follow, we do not choose between these two alternatives. We try to imagine what physical and social situations might have caused the psalmists to sing and pray, but we also appreciate the different dimensions of the spiritual situations of the various psalmists.

As was noted in chapter 2, the most common type of psalm is the prayer for help, which finds its life situation in times of trouble. These psalms complain, mourn, and cry out to God for help. There are many reasons given for the need for help, different life situations that give rise to the psalm. Within this genre of psalm and the accompanying life situations personified in the prayers for help, there is a predominant issue that is raised again and again: the struggle with enemies.

*"I am" separated, distant, lonely, attacked.* Psalm 25 offers an excellent example of the psalmist beset by enemies and separated from the community:

> Turn to me and be gracious to me,
>     for I am lonely and afflicted.
> Relieve the troubles of my heart,
>     and bring me out of my distress.
> Consider my affliction and my trouble,
>     and forgive all my sins.
>
> Consider how many are my foes,
>     and with what violent hatred they hate me.
> O guard my life, and deliver me;
>     do not let me be put to shame, for I take refuge in you. (vv. 16–20)

Psalm 25 is an acrostic poem—each verse beginning with a consecutive letter of the Hebrew alphabet—that details the conflict of the righteous person with his enemy. At the center of the psalm (vv. 8–14) a covenant relationship with God is outlined. This central portion of the psalm is the foundation on which the rest of the psalm is structured. On either side of this covenantal center are two requests, one for instruction (vv. 4–7) and one for deliverance from the enemy (vv. 15–18). On either side of these sections is a pair of comparisons of the righteous with the enemy (vv. 1–3 and vv. 19–21). Not only is the poem an acrostic; it is also set up in a chiastic pattern, with parallel passages flanking the center:

7. Claus Westermann, *Praise and Lament in the Psalms* (Atlanta: John Knox, 1981), 24.

A  tension: the righteous and the enemy (vv. 1–3)

  B  instruction: "Make me to know your ways" (vv. 4–7)

    C  covenant theology (vv. 8–14)

  B′  deliverance: "Turn to me and be gracious" (vv. 15–18)

A′  tension: the righteous and the enemy (vv. 19–21)[8]

The summary above, of the psalmist's need and feelings of loneliness, presents a reality that is troubled and unsure. But at the heart of the psalm is another aspect of the life situation. The hope and trust of the psalmist in the covenant relationship he enjoys with God is the anchor on which the psalm is based. The life situation feels dire, but there is confidence as well.

Psalm 140, another of the prayers for help, begins with a plea for deliverance from enemies:

> Deliver me, O LORD, from evildoers;
>   protect me from those who are violent,
> who plan evil things in their minds
>   and stir up wars continually.
> They make their tongue sharp as a snake's,
>   and under their lips is the venom of vipers. (vv. 1–3)

This psalm, which can be imagined as set in a dispute between members of the community, characterizes the psalmist's enemies as "slanderers" (v. 11), as evil plotters (v. 9), and as "arrogant" (v. 5).

The primary weapon of these enemies is slander; their words are sharper than a serpent's tongue. Only in turning to God for support, in taking his case to the one who is the defender of the cause of the needy (v. 12), does the psalmist find hope. The psalmist is facing false witnesses and those who persecute him verbally. The only recourse the psalmist has is, in the words of the psalm, to cry out to God.

This common life social situation of being slandered finds the psalmist, as often as not, feeling herself to be persona non grata. This familiar legal expression, meaning "an unwelcome person," is a fitting label for the setting of many of these psalms. Loneliness, separation from the community, leaves the persona of the psalm reflecting a sense of isolation that is readily identifiable.

As was observed in Psalm 25 (and is true of almost all the prayers for help), a vital part of the life situation of the psalmist is the spiritual dimension of trust

---

8. Cf. Samuel L. Terrien, *The Psalms: Strophic Structure and Theological Commentary* (Grand Rapids: Eerdmans, 2003).

in God amid suffering. In the prayer for help, right alongside the complaint, is confidence and trust. The life situation of the psalmist, however serious, is not without hope, because God listens. Psalm 3 follows its complaint with the following expression of confidence:

> But you, O Lord, are a shield around me,
>   my glory, and the one who lifts up my head.
> I cry aloud to the Lord,
>   and he answers me from his holy hill.
>
> I lie down and sleep;
>   I wake again, for the Lord sustains me.
> I am not afraid of ten thousands of people
>   who have set themselves against me all around. (vv. 3–6)

The life situation of the psalmist is reimagined here with the psalmist holding the fact that he is sustained by God as a reason for confidence.

Psalm 28 arises out of a similar tension. The psalmist cries out to God for help and fears that God does not hear:

> Do not refuse to hear me,
> for if you are silent to me,
>   I shall be like those who go down to the Pit. (v. 1b)

Again the wicked are all around, characterized as two-faced and fork-tongued, "speaking peace" while plotting "mischief" (v. 3). Following quickly on the heels of this plea for God not to be silent, the psalmist reframes his life situation, declaring that God has indeed heard his prayer:

> Blessed be the Lord,
>   for he has heard the sound of my pleadings.
> The Lord is my strength and my shield;
>   in him my heart trusts;
> so I am helped, and my heart exults,
>   and with my song I give thanks to him. (vv. 6–7)

Because the psalmist is heard, the psalmist is helped.

The life situations reflected in these psalms are not difficult to imagine. In each case the psalm itself will show the reader what the issues are: there are enemies all around, the psalmist has sinned and begs forgiveness, there are those who speak against the "I" of the psalm, and so forth. Alongside the all-too-frequent reality that the psalmist's enemies are around about him comes the affirmation that God does answer prayer. These are the dueling banjos of the theology of the psalms: real-life trouble on the one hand, answered by confidence in God's grace on the other hand. The life situation of most of the psalms reflects this balance for each reader, inviting us to understand our own experiences in this way.

Adopting the persona of a given psalm, "putting ourselves in the psalmist's shoes," is not only an effective way to understand how the psalm creates meaning (or how humans use the psalms to create meaning in their lives) and what it is about, but may also be the central rhetorical force of the psalms. The individual is confronted amid life situations and experiences that demand attention: more than merely inviting one in, they seem to draw one in. Such a reading requires relating the psalmist's life situation to our own. This is an act of imagination, inspired by the nature of the persona and the life situations presented to the reader in the psalm.

To this point we have emphasized likeness, pointing to the many cases in which the life situation of the psalms may resonate with that of the reader; yet this is not always the case. Some life situations reflected in the psalms are not easily appropriated, and the modern reader may be forced to struggle. Psalm 137 is a classic example of a psalm reflecting a life situation that often causes modern readers to shrink back or have a sense of discomfort. As you read this psalm, pay attention to your own emotions. Do you resonate with the emotions of the psalm? Or do you flinch away from its emotions?

> ¹ By the rivers of Babylon—
>     there we sat down and there we wept
>     when we remembered Zion.
> ² On the willows there
>     we hung up our harps.
> ³ For there our captors
>     asked us for songs,
> and our tormentors asked for mirth, saying,
>     "Sing us one of the songs of Zion!"
>
> ⁴ How could we sing the LORD's song
>     in a foreign land?
> ⁵ If I forget you, O Jerusalem,
>     let my right hand wither!
> ⁶ Let my tongue cling to the roof of my mouth,
>     if I do not remember you,
> if I do not set Jerusalem
>     above my highest joy.

⁷Remember, O LORD, against the Edomites
     the day of Jerusalem's fall,
how they said, "Tear it down! Tear it down!
     Down to its foundations!"
⁸O daughter Babylon, you devastator!
     Happy shall they be who pay you back
     what you have done to us!
⁹Happy shall they be who take your little ones
     and dash them against the rock!

For many readers, hearing a prayer in which the pray-er requests that one's oppressors' children die is emotionally and ethically difficult, to say the least. The final verses may well leave one cold—and this may be a good thing. This is a harsh phrase, and it can be hard to read. In fact, many Christian hymn-books that include the psalms have tended to leave this one out for precisely these reasons. So is it impossible to read this psalm, to try to understand the setting in life which might give rise to such harsh language?

## BY THE RIVERS OF BABYLON

Zion psalms, as songs, still resonate, even when the message is hard. Consider Psalm 137. Hasidic reggae artist Matisyahu (Matthew Paul Miller) has a haunting and powerful song called "Jerusalem," which is essentially a reimaging and reclaiming, in a new context and time, of what it means to sing this song of Zion. Matisyahu sings,

> Jerusalem, if I forget you,
> Fire not gonna come from me tongue.

Where the psalm talks about the ability to sing the "songs of Zion" being literally, physically stopped up because of the psalmist's situation ("Let my tongue stick to the roof of my mouth" [v. 6 AT]), Matisyahu puts it in terms of his ability to "spit fire," to tell the truth, powerfully, in his rhymes. The song goes on to draw connections across a range of times and experiences, from the suffering of the people in the Babylonian exile, to the trials of three thousand years of persecution, to the concentration camps, to the loss of Jewish identity in the face of anti-Semitism in Western culture.

In a similar way, the Rastafari group the Melodians released a song called "The Rivers of Babylon" (1970, later covered by Sublime in 1992), which is an appropriation of Psalm 137, with a bit of Psalm 19 thrown in:

> By the rivers of Babylon, there we sat down . . .
> Now how shall we sing the Lord's song in a strange land?

There are a number of things a reader needs to think about in order to understand the emotions of this psalm. Who is this who is singing, and who are the captors? What is a song of Zion? Who are the Edomites? What is Babylon, and why does the psalmist attack it so viciously?

The life situation of the psalm is that of Israelites who have been taken away into captivity by the Babylonian Empire sometime around 586 BCE, following the defeat of Judah, the fall of Jerusalem, and the destruction of the temple. There, separated from their God's place of worship, they are tormented by the victorious Babylonians who urge them to sing their national (and theological) songs. The Edomites were the Israelites' neighbors and supposed allies, who seem to have switched sides and taken part in the destruction of Jerusalem. There, in slavery and defeat, the psalmist sings. Because of the psalmist's reference to "our harps" and "songs" and "my right hand" (with which one strums a harp), we can imagine the singer as a former temple musician, forced into exile in Babylon and mockingly asked to sing a song about Zion (the temple in Jerusalem).

While the words of the psalm may not be words one would want to take up for oneself, they are words that can be understood. Feeling their defeat, suffering mockery, having witnessed the deaths of loved ones, and unable to understand their separation from God, such harsh language can be understood—even if not embraced.

A note of encouragement and warning: reading the psalms is an act of imagination and requires an active imagination. Not every life situation reflected in the psalms will make perfect sense to the modern reader. What this means is that in order to understand the psalms, there are times when it is necessary to try to suspend our judgments. A lack of imagination can make reading the difficult material in the psalms even more difficult.

## The Temple and Israelite Religion as Background of the Psalms

In addition to the life situations of psalms that one may discern from their content, a number of psalms provide an explicit setting for which the psalm was written. The use of the psalms in worship in the temple is known from texts such as 1 Chronicles 16 and is reflected in the superscriptions of a number of psalms both in relation to authorship and rubrics for worship.

There are several ways in which the use of the psalms in some worship setting becomes clear. The life situation of the psalm in worship is shown through the superscriptions that characterize certain psalms as directed to a particular temple official, or as to be sung to a particular musical setting,

## THE STAR-SPANGLED BANNER

O say can you see by the dawn's early light,
What so proudly we hailed at the twilight's last gleaming,
Whose broad stripes and bright stars through the perilous fight,
O'er the ramparts we watched, were so gallantly streaming?
And the rockets' red glare, the bombs bursting in air,
Gave proof through the night that our flag was still there;
O say does that star-spangled banner yet wave,
O'er the land of the free and the home of the brave?

When Americans think of "The Star-Spangled Banner," what life setting is most likely to come to mind? Many people might think of the start of a sporting event, because that is the setting where people most often hear or sing the anthem. People might picture the players lined up neatly on the sideline, some of them trying to shake off nervous jitters, others inwardly focusing, others looking bored. Similarly, people might think of an Olympic medal ceremony. They might picture three proud athletes standing on a trilevel podium, with flags being raised and the anthem of the gold-medal winner playing.

But people might also think of the original life situation that stirred Francis Scott Key to pen the anthem. Key wrote the poem in 1814, during the conflict known as the War of 1812. Held overnight on a British warship outside Baltimore, Key observed a nighttime bombardment of that city's defenses. Key did not know the outcome of the bombardment until morning, when he saw a large flag flying above Fort McHenry.

Inspired by the sight, Key used the back of a letter and began to write a poem that he titled "The Defense of Fort McHenry." Later the poem was set to a popular melody.

Consider the following questions:

- Does knowledge of the original life setting of the poem contribute to the meaning of the song? How or how not?
- Does it make a difference to know that the flag Key saw flying had fifteen stars and fifteen stripes? Or do most modern audiences think of the contemporary flag when they sing the song?
- What might a former gold-medal athlete think of when hearing the song? Or a current high school band director? How does one's job affect how the poem means?
- How does the change of titles from "The Defense of Fort McHenry" to "The Star-Spangled Banner" change the meaning?
- Key's original poem had four stanzas. Have you ever heard or sung any of those other stanzas?

or as for a particular moment in the life of the nation. Another indication of the use to which a psalm may have been put arises from the language or structure of the psalm itself. Finally, the attribution of two particular collections of psalms suggests a close relationship between the psalms and the temple musicians whose name they bear.

Fifty-five psalms are introduced with a Hebrew phrase that means "to the leader" or perhaps "to the choir director."[9] The most likely meaning of this phrase is that the psalms were intended—at least in secondary usage—to be sung by singers in worship. Many of these same psalms are also given other headings that indicate either instrumentation to accompany the singing of the psalm or perhaps liturgical settings or forms in which the psalm was recited or sung. Each of Psalms 54; 55; 61; 67; and 76 are to be performed in worship "with stringed instruments." Several psalms offer cryptic terms that are musical or liturgical in nature, but in just what sense we cannot know: Psalms 45; 69; and 80 are set to "the lilies"; Psalms 8; 81; and 84 to "the gittith"; Psalm 22 is "according to the deer of the dawn"; and Psalms 5; 53; and 88 are "according to Mahalath." It is impossible to say just what each of the technical terms meant, or how the musical accompaniment would have sounded, but that the psalms are set for singing in worship seems clear.

Another indicator of the settings of several psalms is their use in an identifiable service of worship. Psalm 100, "a psalm of thanksgiving," may have been intended for use at the Festival of Tabernacles (cf. Exod. 23:16–17). Psalms 38 and 70 are dedicated to "the memorial offering." As was mentioned earlier in this chapter, Psalm 30 has a superscription that says, "A Song at the dedication of the temple." The word "dedication" in Hebrew is *ḥanukkah*—so perhaps the song was intended in its secondary usage to be sung at the Jewish festival of Hanukkah. Here again it should be recognized that exactly how thanks, memorial, and dedication shape the meaning of the psalm is open to some interpretation. As an example, Psalm 70, which was at some point connected to the "memorial offering," says nothing explicitly about such an offering:

> [1] Be pleased, O God, to deliver me.
>     O Lord, make haste to help me!
> [2] Let those be put to shame and confusion
>     who seek my life.
> Let those be turned back and brought to dishonor
>     who desire to hurt me.

---

9. Some scholars reject this translation, saying that the verbal form of the word has to do with light shining; for example, see Mowinckel, *Psalms in Israel's Worship*, 213. However, the sense of musical leadership in worship is clear in 1 Chron. 15:21 and 23:4 as well as in Ezra 3:8–9.

³ Let those who say, "Aha, Aha!"
        turn back because of their shame.
⁴ Let all who seek you
        rejoice and be glad in you.
Let those who love your salvation
        say evermore, "God is great!"
⁵ But I am poor and needy;
        hasten to me, O God!
You are my help and my deliverer;
        O Lord, do not delay!

Is the memorial offering connected in this case to a sin offering? Is it an attempt to draw God's attention to the conflict with the neighbor? Or is it primarily a part of the call for help? The reader must leave the question open at this point since the psalm does not give a clear indication of what the term means.

In addition to technical terminology in the superscriptions, within the body of several psalms are also indications of liturgical patterns or actions tied to worship, involving festal shouts and calls to praise.

Psalm 81:3 calls Israel to worship, saying, "Blow the trumpet at the new moon, at the full moon, on our festal day." The psalm connects this call with celebratory acts of worship: singing aloud, shouting for joy, raising a song to the sound of the tambourine, the lyre, and the harp (vv. 1–2). This festival celebration is described as a "decree" or command that has its roots in the exodus event, "when [God] went out over the land of Egypt" (v. 5). Worship on this particular day is to celebrate the wonders that God has done for Israel in the past and to remember them. The life setting is not only in worship but also in the theological remembrance of Israel's story.

Psalm 42 centers the prayer for help in the context of worship. The psalm-ist, as he struggles with his illness and is unable to go to the temple, longs for the time when he was with God's people in worship:

> These things I remember,
>     as I pour out my soul:
> how I went with the throng,
>     and led them in procession to the house of God,
> with glad shouts and songs of thanksgiving,
>     a multitude keeping festival. (v. 4)

The force of this particular psalm is in the disconnect the psalmist feels be-tween the imagination of a "proper life situation" (singing in the temple with friends and colleagues) and the current life situation: living in lonely exile among foreigners and strangers. The remembrance of the psalmist's days in worship, in the house of God—the temple—are meant to serve as encouragement and hope for the present.

Psalm 89:15 sounds a similar note in a similar way:

> Happy are the people who know the festal shout,
> who walk, O LORD, in the light of your countenance.

These are but a few of the examples of worship-specific language found in the body of the psalms, tying the expression of the life of faith in all its complexity to the place of worship.

The point here is that an engaged reading of the psalms can be helped by some digging into the ancient Israelite religious background of the psalms. The competent reader needs imagination, as we have said. And a reader's imagination about possible life situations for various psalms will be helped by digging into some of the terms, practices, and social realities that were current during the period in which the psalms were composed.

As a final example, consider the psalms of Asaph and of the Korahites. These psalms have already been discussed in this chapter's excursus "Understanding the Psalm Superscriptions," so there is no need to go into detail here other than to note that Asaph and Korah are mentioned in Chronicles as playing central roles in the worship that King David established when he brought the ark of the covenant to Jerusalem. Although Chronicles is one of the later traditions in the Old Testament, the information found there does suggest that at a relatively early date the psalms of Asaph and of the Korahites were connected explicitly to worship. Thus, Chronicles invites us to imagine temple worship as one of the life situations of some of the psalms.

## The Congregation and the Individual in the Psalms

Are the psalms written for individual use or for the congregation as a whole? As with many such questions, the answer depends in large part on whom one asks, because the answer is yes. The psalms were and are a part of corporate worship. The psalms were and are also read by individuals. What is striking about the psalms themselves is that they seem to be written with this dual usage in mind.

The congregation appears in several places in the psalms but rarely if ever without the individual in mind. Psalm 74 calls on God:

Remember your congregation, which you acquired long ago,
 which you redeemed to be the tribe of your heritage. (v. 2)

Psalm 111:1 locates the praise of the individual within the context of the congregation:

I will give thanks to the LORD with my whole heart,
 in the company of the upright, in the congregation.

This is a motif that is repeated frequently in the psalms (cf. Pss. 1:5; 22:22; 40:9–10; 107:32).

What is more, there are several psalms that intentionally connect the individual with the congregation, in a sense making the life situation the heritage of any who reads them. Consider the following examples:

### Psalm 78:1–5

Give ear, O my people, to my teaching;
 incline your ears to the words of my mouth.
I will open my mouth in a parable;
 I will utter dark sayings from of old,
things that we have heard and known,
 that our ancestors have told us.
We will not hide them from their children;
 we will tell to the coming generation
the glorious deeds of the LORD, and his might,
 and the wonders that he has done.

He established a decree in Jacob,
 and appointed a law in Israel,
which he commanded our ancestors
 to teach to their children.

### Psalm 85:1–8

LORD, you were favorable to your land;
 you restored the fortunes of Jacob.
You forgave the iniquity of your people;
 you pardoned all *their* sin.
You withdrew all your wrath;
 you turned from your hot anger.

Restore *us* again, O God of our salvation,
 and put away your indignation toward us.
Will you be angry with us forever?
 Will you prolong your anger to all generations?

## POOR WAYFARING STRANGER

Read the following poem and think what kind of "I" (or persona) you imagine, simply based on the lyrics.

> I'm just a poor wayfaring stranger,
> I'm traveling through this world of woe;
> Yet there's no sickness, toil nor danger
> In that bright land to which I go.
> I'm going there to see my father,
> I'm going there no more to roam,
> I'm only going over Jordan,
> I'm only going over home.
>
> I know dark clouds will gather 'round me,
> I know my way is rough and steep,
> Yet golden fields lie just before me
> Where God's redeemed shall ever sleep.
> I'm going there to see my mother;
> She said she'd meet me when I come;
> I'm only going over Jordan,
> I'm only going over home.

In the first stanza, the singer sings, "I'm going there to see my father." What kind of father do you imagine? What might one imagine has happened so that the singer cannot see one's father? What journey is the song talking about? What is the destination the singer hopes to reach?

The composer (or composers) of this folk song is unknown. The song originated in nineteenth-century America among African American slaves. Recall that it was not unknown for slave families to be broken up when they were sold: father and mother and child might be wrenched apart. How does that awful reality change how one interprets the song?

The main metaphor of the song is that the singer is a "poor wayfaring stranger." How does one interpret that metaphor? It is also likely that the anonymous slaves who composed this song drew on Psalm 39:12 when they came up with this metaphor:

> Hear my prayer, O LORD,
>     and give ear unto my cry;
>     hold not thy peace at my tears:
> For I am a stranger with thee,
>     and a sojourner, as all my fathers were. (KJV)

Notice the words "stranger" and "fathers" in these lines. Does the connection between the song and the psalm contribute to the song's meaning?

Will you not revive us again,
    so that your people may rejoice in you?
Show us your steadfast love, O Lord,
    and grant us your salvation.

Let *me* hear what God the Lord will speak,
    for he will speak peace to his people, to his faithful,
    to those who turn to him in their hearts. (emphasis added)

### Psalm 106:4–7, 47–48

Remember me, O Lord, when you show favor to your people;
    help me when you deliver them;
that I may see the prosperity of your chosen ones,
    that I may rejoice in the gladness of your nation,
    that I may glory in your heritage.

Both we and our ancestors have sinned;
    we have committed iniquity, have done wickedly.
Our ancestors, when they were in Egypt,
    did not consider your wonderful works;
they did not remember the abundance of your steadfast love,
    but rebelled against the Most High at the Red Sea.

. . . . . . . . . . . . . . . . . . . . . . . . . . . . . . . . . . . . . . . . .

Save us, O Lord our God,
    and gather us from among the nations,
that we may give thanks to your holy name
    and glory in your praise.

Blessed be the Lord, the God of Israel,
    from everlasting to everlasting.
And let all the people say, "Amen."
    Praise the Lord!

In each of these psalms there is movement from I, to we, to they, and back again. Their sins are my sins. Remember me when you remember them. I will tell what we know that our ancestors have told us. The sense in these psalms is that the persona, the figure presented by the psalm, is available for readers to adopt as well. The life situation in these psalms is passed on as appropriate to the reader, and perhaps more than appropriate, as essential. The individual is made the pray-er as the psalm places words in the mouth of the one who is praying:

You who live in the shelter of the Most High,
    who abide in the shadow of the Almighty,

will say to the LORD, "My refuge and my fortress;
    my God, in whom I trust." (91:1–2)

## Conclusion

The concept of persona arises not only out of attributed authorship but also out of a sense that the psalm is meant to be tried out and tried on by the reader. The psalms are often ambiguous, and intentionally so; thus, the reader is not limited in applying a situation of trouble or an occasion of celebration, or responding to the summons to join in the festal shouts that the psalmist first employs. Persona and life situation are two sides of the same interpretive coin, which make the meaning of the psalm accessible and the use of the psalm not only possible but also appropriate.

### ───── GOING DEEPER ─────

In order to deepen your grasp of the concepts introduced in this chapter, consider doing one or more of the following exercises:

1. Open up a Bible and read one of the following psalms: 13; 25; 51; 91. Now write your own version of the psalm, putting yourself in the shoes of the psalmist but using your own words.
2. What kind of person would write a psalm such as 137? Can you imagine yourself speaking or praying from such a dark and angry place? What would your vengeance psalm sound like?
3. Listen to your favorite song. How is listening to a song similar to reading a psalm? How does a song—its lyrics, its energy, its artist—speak to you personally? What kind of psalm speaks to you in this way?

### ───── FOR FURTHER READING ─────

Brueggemann, Walter. *The Psalms and the Life of Faith*. Minneapolis: Fortress, 1995.

McCann, J. Clinton. *A Theological Introduction to the Book of Psalms*. Nashville: Abingdon, 1993.

Miller, Patrick D. *Interpreting the Psalms*. Philadelphia: Fortress, 1986.

Westermann, Claus. *Praise and Lament in the Psalms*. Louisville: Westminster John Knox, 1987.

FIVE

# Is God a Rock, a Light, or a Shepherd?

*Learning to Understand Metaphors, Imagery, and Symbolism in the Psalms*

## Introducing the Concept of Metaphor

Is God a rock, a shepherd, or a hiding place? Are human beings sheep, trees, or worms? Is God's Word a lamp, plunder, or the way? These questions, posed in figurative language, are central to the way the poetry of the biblical psalms makes its theological, religious, and spiritual hay. All of these are, of course, metaphors. And metaphors are central to how the psalms, which are often such tiny pieces of literature, can pack such a powerful punch. As Pierre Van Hecke puts it, "Not only are metaphors a characteristic part of Hebrew poetry's stylistics; . . . metaphor [is also] a way of conceptualizing reality. More than a matter of style or language, metaphor—and figurative speech in general—is a matter of thinking."[1] Which is to say, *metaphorical thinking is psalmic thinking.*

1. Pierre Van Hecke and Antje Labahn, eds. *Metaphors in the Psalms* (Leuven: Peeters, 2010), xii.

---

### WHAT *ISN'T* GOD?

In a moving reflection on matters of life and death, faith and doubt, titled "Seven Psalms," Paul Simon engages in a series of unique metaphors for his wrestling with God. Here is a sample:

> The Lord is my engineer
> The Lord is the earth I ride on

The metaphors pile up, one after the other, throughout the seven "movements" of the piece. For example, the Lord is, consecutively, a face that appears in the atmosphere, both the forest and the ranger who cares for it, a meal for the poor, a welcoming door for strangers, and, perhaps most provocatively of all, "my personal joke."

---

The metaphors employed in the psalms are *a* (maybe *the*) principal point of contact that many readers have with the psalms. Metaphor directly engages the imagination of the reader; it makes possible both understanding the message of the psalms and connecting with the point of the psalms.

Try this whole metaphor thing out for yourself with this word challenge. Pick something or someone important to you, maybe your father, mother, a friend, or significant other; perhaps your favorite sports team, music group, or television show. Do you have this in mind? Imagine that you are given the task of explaining to a classmate or friend how important that person or thing is to you, but you may use only twenty words or less. One way to try to meet this word challenge would be to use a metaphor or two. You could say, "My mother is . . . [insert a metaphor or two here that accurately communicates your mother's finer qualities]." Or, you might say, "To me, the Minnesota Vikings have been . . . [insert here a metaphor or two that communicate the endless frustration of cheering for a team that never wins it all]."

Do you see how a metaphor works? In the psalms, the authors use metaphors to help readers picture and understand many different aspects of the life of faith: ourselves, our communities, other people, and, above all, God.

### Interpreting Metaphors and Imagery

So just what is a metaphor? A metaphor is a picture that is painted in words. That sentence *was* a metaphor! A metaphor is described in terms of the image of a painting.

Metaphorical language is essentially representative in nature: one thing (usually something that is less easily known or less fully understood) is represented as something else (usually something that is quite familiar and that is well understood). In a metaphor, a basic semantic comparison is made where "A" is expressed by "B" and yet "B" cannot literally be the "A" it represents. "The LORD is my shepherd" is a famous example of a metaphor in the psalms. More on metaphors in a moment.

A separate but related issue is imagery. Imagery, too, is central to both how the psalms make meaning and to all meaning. We deal in imagery and symbols on a daily basis—and we depend on the meaning of imagery and symbols in many ways. Here are a few simple examples to make the point. What might this image represent?

In the United States, where this shape is seen on street corners, painted red and white, the octagon represents "stop." Even without the full image—without the sign being painted red, with the white word "stop" in the center—most people in our culture would likely assign the meaning "stop" to the above image. But notice something: this meaning is culturally specific. People from other cultures may not assign the meaning "stop" to the sign. In Japan, the stop sign is an inverted, red triangle. In other places a stop sign can be round with a white horizontal line.

So, when interpreting an image from another culture, a competent reader dare not assume that the meaning one's own culture assigns to an image or symbol is the same as that which someone from the original culture would assign to a symbol.

When it comes to interpreting the Bible, for instance, in the Old Testament the "shepherd" was a royal symbol: people in Israel or in cultures close to Israel would normally assume that the "shepherd" referred to the king. Thus, in Ezekiel 34, the prophet prophesies against "the shepherds of Israel" (v. 1), meaning the kings. But by New Testament times, the culture had changed. In the Greco-Roman culture of the New Testament era, the shepherd was not a valued occupation, and shepherds were generally looked down on by other people. So when the birth of the Messiah is announced to "shepherds living in the fields, keeping watch over their flock by night" (Luke 2:8), the original audience would not assign royal meaning to these characters. They might have found it odd that such grand news was first shared not with the king in Jerusalem but with lowly shepherds in the fields.

Back to metaphors. Metaphors employ language to create what we might call "word pictures" or "verbal symbols." These pictures and symbols *signify one thing in terms of another*. That is, they signify something about one thing (for example, God) in terms of another thing (for example, "light" or "a fortress" or "a shepherd").

As indicated above, one of the problems with gestures and pictures is that their meaning is not necessarily universal, meaning the same thing in every culture. The hand gestures for "come over here" are entirely different in China, for example, than in the United States. If you travel to China and try crooking your index finger at someone to get them to come over to you, you are as likely to get a slap in the face as not. Wave what you think is "good-bye," and a Chinese person will not walk away but will come over to you. Gestures and signs are not universal: they are culturally conditioned. The same is true for metaphors. Not every image, as described in a psalm, will be readily understood by the reader. Though metaphor is an important and basic way in which the ancient poetry is made available for a modern reader by engaging the imagination,[2] that imagination will still require some exercise.

When seeking to understand a metaphor, there are two basic elements that need to be considered: the two parts of the metaphor. First, one needs to consider the *thing being described*, and second, one needs to consider *the thing used to describe the first thing*. In the study of metaphor, these two different things are called "target domain" and "source domain," respectively.[3] For example, in the phrase "The LORD is my light" (Ps. 27:1), "the LORD" is the target domain and "light" is the source domain. In the psalms there are many different subjects of the metaphor, from God, to various human beings (the righteous, the wicked, the enemy, and others), to life situations (some

2. William P. Brown, *Seeing the Psalms: A Theology of Metaphor* (Louisville: Westminster John Knox, 2002), 28.

3. See George Lakoff and Mark Turner, *More Than Cool Reason: A Field Guide to Poetic Metaphor* (Chicago: University of Chicago Press, 1989). Lakoff and Turner's terms replace the older "vehicle" and "tenor" terms. For the best development of the metaphorical theory in relation to the Psalms, see Brown, *Seeing the Psalms*, esp. the introduction and chaps. 1–2.

good and some bad), to God's Word, and so on. The source domains from which these various target domains are described are equally varied, such as agricultural ("grass"), geographic ("mountain" or "rock"), architectural ("fortress" or "dwelling place"), celestial ("light" and "darkness"), and many other source domains.

What makes metaphors evocative and powerful is that the object almost always comes from a different realm than the subject. Consider the following from Psalm 18:46: "The LORD lives! Blessed be my rock." Here God is called "my rock." The target or subject of the metaphor is "the LORD." The object of the metaphor, the source image, is from the natural realm of creation, a rock. Is the psalm saying that God is literally a rock? Of course not—unless the Lord is actually The Thing from the Fantastic Four. The two phrases that make up this half verse do not go together in any literal way that makes sense. The Lord lives, after all, and rocks do not. So how can the Lord be a rock? Interpretive imagination is needed to make sense of what it means to think of God as a "rock." Imagining God as a rock brings to mind stability (cf. 40:2), protection (cf. 18:2), or surety and reliability (cf. 92:15).

Again, imagination is required to understand a metaphor. But one should not just let one's imagination run completely wild and free. The imagination should also be informed by a little investigative digging into the ancient cultural background of the society that produced the psalms. The reason for this, as mentioned earlier in this chapter, is that all images are embedded in particular cultures; thus, when one communicates via metaphor across cultural boundaries, from one culture to another, misunderstanding can occur (as illustrated above, with the hand wave in China).

## METAPHOR AS REIMAGINATION

In 2007 Doubleday published *The Manga Bible: From Genesis to Revelation*, by Ajinbayo Akinsiku (Siku). The text is identified in the introduction as a "first-step" into the biblical material. The work is a sort of hybrid text employing narration, quotation, and images to "tell the story of God's relationship with his people."[a]

When it comes to the book of Psalms, there is only one page, and the psalm chosen to represent the psalms is Psalm 18. The representation of Psalm 18 is a composite of a few words and a panel of eight images. The "quotation" of Psalm 18:34, 46 is quite close to the actual biblical text, but the image is of a man carrying two automatic weapons. The visual anachronism is an attempt to modernize the psalm and to reimagine the application of the text.

a. Ajinbayo Akinsiku, *The Manga Bible: From Genesis to Revelation* (New York: Doubleday, 2007), v.

Let us tackle the ancient Israelite "cultural embeddedness" of the term "rock." As we try to wrap our minds around what the phrase means, we might wonder what meaning ancient Israelites might have associated with the metaphor. Would they have thought of a little rock, one that you could throw with a sling as a weapon? Would they have thought of a bigger rock, one that you could jump up on to flee from a charging ox? Or would they have thought of a mountain, one where you could build a fortress that would protect you from an invading army? Would the image have been primarily positive, meaning that God is reliable, trustworthy, or a refuge in times of trouble? Or would the image have been primarily negative, meaning that God is deaf to our cries (like a rock) or is a stumbling block (something we trip over)? The reader who starts to imagine those sorts of questions is engaging in the sort of imaginative questioning the metaphors of the psalms call for.

The competent reader would then wonder how one chooses wisely between the various options. How can one decide which of the above options—if any—offers the best answer to the question? In order to answer this question, one must search through a set of parallel or comparative texts that also use the term "rock" in order to find clues as to what the term "rock" may mean. When reading the psalms, these parallel or comparative texts might include other psalms, other passages in the Old Testament, any available art from ancient Israel, any literary passages or visual art from cultures that were ancient Israel's neighbors, and other passages from the long tradition of interpretation. With regard to what "my rock" means in Psalm 18, these other passages from the book of Psalms might provide some help:

> You are indeed my rock and my fortress;
>     for your name's sake lead me and guide me. (31:3)

> He drew me up from the desolate pit,
>     out of the miry bog,
> and set my feet upon a rock,
>     making my steps secure. (40:2)

> Be to me a rock of refuge,
>     a strong fortress, to save me,
>         for you are my rock and my fortress. (71:3)

> The high mountains are for the wild goats;
>     the rocks are a refuge for the coneys. (104:18)

This set of parallel or comparative texts offers context and a set of clues that help an interpreter understand what the poem might mean when calling God "my rock." On the one hand (from a positive sense), these texts suggest that the interpretation that best fits what the psalmist in Psalm 18 means when calling God "my rock" seems to be something along the lines of a "rock big enough to hold a fortress" or "a firm foundation on which to stand." On the other hand (from a negative sense), these texts suggest that the psalmist certainly does *not* mean "a small rock that one can hurl with a sling" or "a stumbling block to trip over."

One final comment about metaphors. As already noted, the way metaphors work is by overlaying or superimposing one concept (from the source domain) over another concept (the target domain). This superimposing says something new about the target domain, doing so by making a connection with some aspect or aspects of the source domain. For example, when Psalm 23 says that the Lord is a shepherd, several aspects from the "shepherd" source domain are connected to the concept of the Lord: the Lord is one who keeps watch, guards, guides, leads to safe and secure places, and so on. But there are other aspects of the "shepherd" source domain that the metaphor does not intend to connect with the concept of the Lord—perhaps that shepherds smell like the sheep they watch, or have long beards, or sleep in tents, or that sort of thing.

For this reason, scholars who study metaphors often say that when a metaphor works, it is both true and not true at the same time. When a metaphor works, the audience makes the right connections that the metaphor wants the reader to make, but at the same time the audience filters out the wrong connections—those connections that the speaker of the metaphor might not want the audience to make. Competent readers of the psalms engage their imagination in such a way that the true or right connections are made as fully as possible, while the wrong or not true connections are filtered out as much as possible.

## Metaphor and the Psalms

Metaphor is central to the way in which the psalms create and communicate meaning. Along with parallelism, metaphor is the essential element not only of Hebrew poetry but also of the Psalms as a whole. The book of Psalms begins with an extended metaphor that invites the reader into the imagination of what life lived on the basis of God's Word might look like.

> [1] Fortunate is the one
>    who does not walk in the advice of the wicked,

who does not stand on the path that sinners tread,
    who does not sit in the seat of scoffers.
² Rather, that one delights in the Torah of the LORD,
    who meditates on his Torah both day and night.
³ This one is like a tree that has been transplanted by streams of water;
    who yields fruit in due season, whose leaves do not wither.
    This one prospers in all that is done.
⁴ Not so the wicked!
    They are like chaff that the wind drives away.
⁵ Therefore the wicked will not stand in the judgment,
    nor sinners in the congregation of the righteous;
⁶ The LORD knows the way of the righteous,
    but the way of the wicked perishes. (Ps. 1 AT)

In Psalm 1 several metaphors are working at the same time. The faithful, who take to heart God's Word and study it, are compared to well-watered trees. In fact, the Hebrew even suggests that they are like trees that were "transplanted" intentionally to be next to the water. The Word of God in this metaphor is likened to water, and the reader of the Word is likened to a tree that is nourished by that water. The metaphor is extended to a comparison as well. The one who is like this will bear good fruit and be healthy, even in dry seasons and through storms. But the wicked ones will be like dry and dusty chaff that blows away, like the leaves that fall from trees in the autumn.

---

### PSALM I IN *HANG 'EM HIGH*

In Clint Eastwood's Western film *Hang 'Em High* (1968), Psalm 1 takes the form of a different sort of antithetical parallelism. As a number of convicted criminals are waiting on the gallows for their sentences to be carried out, "The Preacher" (played by James MacArthur) recites Psalm 1, which is usually taken as a guidepost for a life of faith, a contrast between two ways, the way of the righteous and the way of the wicked. Clearly, Psalm 1 invites the reader to a righteous and fruitful life. In the film, the psalm is read at a hanging, haltingly and uncomfortably, and its impact is markedly different, emphasizing the fate of the wicked, who "are like chaff that the wind drives away" (v. 4). The psalm here serves not as an invitation to a fruitful life but as a judgment over an unfruitful one. What this then does is invite the viewer to a different experience of the psalm, a different entry into reflection, which nevertheless invites the same question: Will one choose happiness, blessedness, and life that grows out of a commitment to the law of the Lord, or will one choose death?

But what does this extended metaphor mean? One way to understand the metaphor is to view it as saying that the rest of the Psalter should be understood as a wellspring of water for the reader. Those who read the psalms will find in them nourishing spiritual water, which will help feed a spiritual life that bears fruit and flourishes even in tough times.

The presence of this metaphor at the heart of Psalm 1 also tips the reader off that metaphors will abound in the poems that follow.

There is also another metaphor central to Psalm 1: the metaphor of "the way" or "the pathway" one takes through life. In the psalm, the way of the

---

## A TREE BY ANY OTHER NAME

Picture a tree. Or better yet, draw a tree.

What kind of tree did you picture or draw?

In order to interpret and understand a metaphor, a reader needs to bring their "A game" to the task of reading (oops, notice we accidentally slipped a "game" metaphor into that sentence). The reader has to contribute imagination to the text. To get a sense of how that works, think about the person who is described in Psalm 1. Psalm 1 begins with these words:

> [1]Fortunate is the one
>      who does not walk in the advice of the wicked,
>      who does not stand on the path that sinners tread,
>      who does not sit in the seat of scoffers.
> [2]Rather, that one delights in the Torah of the LORD,
>      who meditates on his Torah both day and night.
> [3]This one is like a tree that has been transplanted by streams of water;
>      who yields fruit in due season, whose leaves do not wither.
>      This one prospers in all that is done. (Ps. 1:1–3 AT)

Imagine the tree of Psalm 1: it is planted by water, it bears fruit, it has leaves that do not wither. How is this tree like or not like the tree you imagined at first? Imagine a typical orange or apple tree. Now, imagine a fig tree, the kind of tree that an ancient Israelite would have known (you might need help: go ahead and google it, using its Latin name *Ficus carica*). Does the psalm have different shades of meaning when you imagine a different kind of fruit tree?

Let us go even deeper to engage this metaphor of the tree. The common fig tree played a critical role in the diet and economy of ancient Israel. One scholar has concluded that "the importance of the fig tree as one of the mainstays of the biblical economy cannot be overemphasized."[a] The tree helped sustain the life of the community. Does knowing this change how one interprets the metaphor of the tree in Psalm 1?

a. Oded Borowski, *Agriculture in Iron Age Israel* (Winona Lake, IN: Eisenbrauns, 1987), 114.

righteous is compared to the way of the wicked ones. The psalm gazes down both paths. The more-traveled pathway—the way taken by the wicked ones, the sinners, and the scoffers—is a way that looks easy at first but leads to destruction. The less-traveled pathway—the way of the righteous—looks lonely at first but is a pathway that leads to a community of faith: to the "congregation of the righteous" (v. 5). The psalm makes a promise: the Lord "knows" the way of the righteous, and God will watch over those who travel life by walking down "the LORD's way." Those who walk down their own paths in life? Well, they go it alone.

There is a subtle promise about interpretation here also: learning to handle metaphors such as "the way" is the way to read the psalms.

As explained above, metaphors are employed in the psalms to represent God and humankind, to reflect on life situations and attitudes, and more. What follows are examples of some of the central metaphorical images in the psalms as they are employed in several major target domains. These are offered here by way of example of how to read the metaphors of the psalms and to offer a map of the types of metaphorical expressions that populate the psalms.

### The Human Situation

The life situation of the psalmist is frequently presented via metaphor. In Psalm 31:12 the suffering of the psalmist has caused separation from the community. The psalmist expresses this separation in terms of one who is (not so) dearly departed:

> I have passed out of mind like one who is dead;
> I have become like a broken vessel.

Note that the psalmist not only imagines his experience as being like a dead man; he also feels useless, a shattered jar that cannot hold anything in. Like the "I am" indicators of life situation discussed in the previous chapter, "I am" statements often lead into a metaphor in the psalms.

Psalm 88 employs similar imagery, the figure of deathlike separation, to express feelings of separation from God:

> I am counted among those who go down to the Pit;
> I am like those who have no help,
> like those forsaken among the dead,
> like the slain that lie in the grave,
> like those whom you remember no more,
> for they are cut off from your hand. (vv. 4–5)

In Psalm 102 the psalmist is suffering as a result of illness and characterizes his lonely suffering in terms of the wild animals of the wilderness:

> I am like an owl of the wilderness,
>     like a little owl of the waste places.
> I lie awake;
>     I am like a lonely bird on the housetop. (vv. 6–7)

The psalmist is not, of course, actually an owl, but the solitary nature of the nocturnal bird mirrors the psalmist's experience of the dark watches of the night.

### Psalmist as Tree or Grass

If you were a tree, what kind of tree would you be? This strange old question, sometimes asked in job interviews to see how quickly a candidate can think, is the most important metaphorical proposition in the psalms. As we have already seen, the Psalter begins by asking this question: Will you be a tree planted by the streams of God's Word or a dry tree unable to stand and blown away like fallen leaves?

In Psalm 52:7–8 the tree is again employed as a comparative metaphor. The psalmist has sought shelter in the temple, and there he has been firmly established and is fruitful:

> "See the one who would not take
>     refuge in God,
> but trusted in abundant riches,
>     and sought refuge in wealth!"
>
> But I am like a green olive tree
>     in the house of God.
> I trust in the steadfast love of God
>     forever and ever.

Unlike the one who trusts only in abundant wealth, the psalmist is a healthy and wealth-giving olive tree.

And Psalm 92 compares the righteous and the wicked:

> The righteous flourish like the palm tree,
>     and grow like a cedar in Lebanon.
> They are planted in the house of the LORD;
>     they flourish in the courts of our God.

> In old age they still produce fruit;
>> they are always green and full of sap,
> showing that the LORD is upright;
>> he is my rock, and there is no unrighteousness in him. (vv. 12–15)

The psalmist is a flourishing, growing tree, planted in proximity to God's house. Earlier in the psalm the wicked are characterized as sprouting all over the place but lasting only as long as grass does:

> Though the wicked sprout like grass and all evildoers flourish,
>> they are doomed to destruction forever. (v. 7)

This image of withering or fading like the grass is another common metaphor in the psalms. The wicked are not pictured as withering before God, but their withering end is prayed for by the psalmist:

> Let them vanish like water that runs away;
>> like grass let them be trodden down and wither. (58:7)

Metaphors of withering things are a favorite source domain that the psalmists borrow from in order to target "the wicked":

> For they will soon fade like the grass,
>> and wither like the green herb. (37:2)

> Let them be like the grass on the housetops
>> that withers before it grows up,
> with which reapers do not fill their hands
>> or binders of sheaves their arms. (129:6–7)

Yet it is not only the wicked that are likened to withering grass; the faithful psalmist sees his illness as a hastening away of his life, as his days fly away:

> For my days pass away like smoke,
>> and my bones burn like a furnace.
> My heart is stricken and withered like grass;
>> I am too wasted to eat my bread. (102:3–4)

> My days are like an evening shadow;
>> I wither away like grass. (102:11)

Time and illness wither the heart of the psalmist, and out of this metaphorical life situation he calls on his God.

Even time is compared to the withering of the grass in the psalms, a metaphor that serves to emphasize the lasting power of God:

> For a thousand years in your sight
> 　are like yesterday when it is past,
> 　or like a watch in the night.
> You sweep them away; they are like a dream,
> 　like grass that is renewed in the morning;
> in the morning it flourishes and is renewed;
> 　in the evening it fades and withers. (90:4–6)

The years are like sleep in the corner of God's eye, dew that dries with the rising of the sun. These metaphors serve to envision the enduring of God, the majesty and timeless power of the creator of time. Like grass with the seasons, so the years come and go before God.

Another powerful image in the psalms is that of sleep. But care must be employed in seeking to understand just how sleep is understood and the way in which it is employed. The continued cycle of waking and lying down to sleep are seen as evidence of God's provision for the psalmist:

> I lie down and sleep;
> 　I wake again, for the LORD sustains me. (3:5; cf. 4:8)

Sleep is also a metaphor for death and dying:

> Give light to my eyes, or I will sleep the sleep of death. (13:3)

And again,

> The stouthearted were stripped of their spoil;
> 　they sank into sleep;
> none of the troops
> 　was able to lift a hand. (76:5)

While in both the psalms and in the wider biblical picture sleep is a metaphor for death, death is not the final word. Sleep and rest are also gifts that God gives to people:

> It is in vain that you rise up early
> 　and go late to rest,
> eating the bread of anxious toil;
> 　for he gives sleep to his beloved. (127:2)

While this last is not a metaphor (at least in its use of "sleep"), it does speak to the nature of sleep and arises out of a related semantic field. Sleep as a metaphor cannot be simply or simplistically read. Sleep, perhaps even the sleep of death, is a part of how God is God in the psalms.

Human living and the situations that one experiences are envisioned in many and various ways in the psalms. Psalm 75:3 talks about the pillars of the earth being shaken and the earth shaking on its perch atop these pillars. God responds to the opening thanksgiving of the psalm:

> When the earth totters, and all its inhabitants,
>    it is I who keep its pillars steady. (AT)

This might be a literal description of an earthquake or of volcanic activity, but in the context of the psalm's attention to the dangers of envy and pride, and the promise of judgment, the image is actually a use of the physical realm's shaking to express the uncertainty and upset in a person's life. This is metaphor at its basic semantic level. Here the disorientation of human life is characterized figuratively in terms borrowed from the natural world, where the earth literally shakes. Again in Psalm 75 the pride of human beings is pictured in pastoral terms as the raising up of the horn, like a proud bull (vv. 4–5). This prideful self-effected horn raising is seen in the psalm as problematic. The close of the psalm claims that God is the one who exalts one horn and cuts off another (v. 10).

Psalm 78 is replete with metaphorical expression. God's anger appears as burning fire (v. 21; cf. 79:5), which finds its outlet or "path" via the wonders God performs in Egypt (v. 50). In the wilderness, where God provides for the hungering people both bread and quail, the psalm recounts mortals eating the "bread of angels" (v. 25) and receiving "rained flesh" from God (v. 27). The fleeting span of human life is "a breath" (v. 33) or "wind that passes" (v. 39). Sinful Israel is pictured as a "deceitful bow" (v. 57 AT), while God is a drunken, slumbering "warrior" (v. 65).

Psalm 73 employs a series of metaphors to describe the relationship of the human being—either the would-be righteous or the wicked—with God. The psalmist describes indulging in envy in terms of perilous footing and stumbling steps (v. 2; see also v. 18). In an implicit way, this picks up the metaphor of life with God as a path. When one strays into sin, and thus off the straight and narrow of God's path, the footing is unsure. In a striking contrast the pride and arrogance of the wicked are pictured as garments: pride is a necklace and violence a cloak (v. 6). These same wicked ones last only as long as a dream, cleared away with the morning's first blinking of the eye (v. 20).

Metaphor is employed variously to describe the human situation and human character. Blood is water poured out on the ground (79:3); sleeplessness is God's holding open the psalmist's eyelids (77:4); the envy of the psalmist is compared to beastly behavior (literally, "Behemoth,"[4] 73:22; "like a brute beast" [NRSV]); the psalmist self-identifies as a "dove" in danger of being devoured by the "wild beasts" who are its enemies (74:19); and Sisera's and Jabin's bodies are "dung for the ground" (83:9–10).

### Metaphor and God

Metaphor in the psalms is not limited to reflection of life situation; metaphor is profoundly theological as well. The psalm that may be the most loved, and also the best known of the psalms, Psalm 23, is an extended mixed metaphor:

> [1] The LORD is my shepherd, I shall not want.
>   [2] He makes me lie down in green pastures;
> he leads me beside still waters;
>   [3] he restores my soul.
> He leads me in right paths
>   for his name's sake.
>
> [4] Even though I walk through the darkest valley,
>   I fear no evil;
> for you are with me;
>   your rod and your staff—
>   they comfort me.
>
> [5] You prepare a table before me
>   in the presence of my enemies;
> you anoint my head with oil;
>   my cup overflows.
> [6] Surely goodness and mercy shall follow me
>   all the days of my life,
> and I shall dwell in the house of the LORD
>   my whole life long.

Notice that this psalm mixes metaphors: the Lord is both a shepherd and a banquet host. If this poem had been written for a high school English course, it would probably have been marked down at least half a grade for mixing metaphors. Is the psalmist a sheep or a house pet? Is God a shepherd

---

4. Brown, *Seeing the Psalms*, 148.

or a host? The answer in the psalm is yes. And thankfully, the psalm was not written for a high school course but for the life of faith.

The overarching metaphor of Psalm 23 is that of provision. God is a provider, like a shepherd who provides for the sheep by leading them to safe pastures, and like a host who provides for the marginalized, giving those who have been shamed and dishonored a place of honor at the spiritual banquet.

But the psalm may also have had both civil and spiritual leadership in mind as well. God is a shepherd, but so is David (cf. Ps. 78:70–71), and Jesus is the "good shepherd" (John 10:11, 14). This particular metaphor of a shepherd may be difficult for some to imagine for themselves. Shepherding is no longer one of the top five professions (probably because there is not a lot of room for advancement), at least not in the Western world. This particular metaphor may take some imagination for us to understand and apprehend for ourselves, particularly if this means that we are the "sheep." But the shepherd imagery has retained a great portion of its strength and can still fire the imagination of the reader if care is taken.

God is not only a shepherd in the psalms; God is also rock, light, fortress, redeemer, and many other things.

By way of example, we will pay sustained attention to one metaphor that the psalms use for God—the metaphor of the rock, which we introduced earlier. Psalm 19, which reflects on the glory of God's Word, ends with an expression of trust in God the rock:

> Let the words of my mouth and the meditation of my heart
>> be acceptable to you,
>> O Lord, my rock and my redeemer. (v. 14)

In fact, on the whole in the psalms, God is more likely to be envisioned as a fortress than as a shepherd or sheepfold. As was noted earlier in this chapter, the idea of God as a rock is only a little less likely than the idea of an insurance company as a rock. But this particular image for God is incredibly common in the psalms.

While many psalms do employ this metaphor of the rock, the two most systematic or sustained engagements of the metaphor are found in Psalms 18 and 62. Psalm 18 uses the metaphor three times as a way of describing how God has provided for the psalmist:

> The Lord is my rock, my fortress, and my deliverer,
>> my God, my rock in whom I take refuge, my shield,
>> and the horn of my salvation, my stronghold. (v. 2)

## A LITTLE WATER NEVER HURT ANYONE

The authors of this book live in the state of Minnesota, which is also known as "the land of ten thousand lakes." Or, in the words of an old advertising jingle, "the land of sky-blue waters." Where we live, water is cherished and loved. It is valued for its beauty. It plays a major role in Minnesota's tourism economy. Many people get away to "the lakes" during the summer for fishing, boating, swimming, and relaxation.

Children are taught to swim, water-ski, and fish at a young age. Our point is that for most Minnesotans, "water" and "the lakes" are words with very positive connotations.

Not so in ancient Israel! For the communities that generated the Psalter, "the waters" and "the sea" carried very threatening connotations. Consider the start of Psalm 69:

> Save me, O God,
>     for the waters have come up to my neck.
> I sink in the miry depths,
>     where there is no foothold.
> I have come into the deep waters;
>     the floods engulf me.
> I am worn out calling for help;
>     my throat is parched.
> My eyes fail,
>     looking for my God. (69:1–3 NIV)

Notice here that the metaphor of "the waters" is an image of absolute terror. The poet who penned these words was drawing on the fact that, for ancient Israel, the "image of overwhelming waters" represented "the embodiment of dynamic forces asserted against God and God's people" and was "an image for death itself."[a] Since the author wrote these words down, we can assume that the author was not literally drowning. Rather, the author of Psalm 69 wanted to communicate a situation of utter terror and thus from the ancient Israelite culture drew on the stock image of "the waters." What this means is that a reader from our culture needs a vibrant imagination to read the psalms. A reader will need to try to imagine a symbolic system that is different from the reader's own symbolic world.

Notice one other detail of the opening verses of Psalm 69: water is both too present and too absent. The waters, depths, deep waters, and floods are (metaphorically) overwhelming the psalm writer. But the psalmist also lacks water: "My throat is parched." The metaphor thus communicates a tragically ironic crisis. The psalmist prays "as if" one were both drowning in water and dying of thirst.

a. John Goldingay, *Psalms 42–89*, vol. 2 of *Psalms* (Grand Rapids: Baker Academic, 2007), 339.

God as rock is protection, deliverance, and so on, but the metaphor is employed as more than simple metaphor; it becomes the theological crux upon
which a claim is made:

> For who is God except the LORD?
>     And who is a rock besides our God? (v. 31)

The incomparability of God is extolled through this metaphor; God is rock,
and no other "god" is such. Finally, perhaps in tension with the discordant
claim that God is a rock, the psalmist declares,

> The LORD lives! Blessed be my rock,
>     and exalted be the God of my salvation. (v. 46)

God is a place of refuge and salvation. In this, God is unlike any other who
might make a claim to godhood or influence in the psalmist's life, particularly
a dead thing . . . like an idol of stone.

In Psalm 62 God is the rock, the only rock in which the psalmist trusts. In
the face of his enemies, the psalmist clings to God:

> For God alone my soul waits in silence;
>     from him comes my salvation.
> He alone is my rock and my salvation,
>     my fortress; I shall never be shaken.
>
> How long will you assail a person,
>     will you batter your victim, all of you,
>         as you would a leaning wall, a tottering fence?
> Their only plan is to bring down a person of prominence.
>     They take pleasure in falsehood;
> they bless with their mouths,
>     but inwardly they curse. (vv. 1–4)

The psalmist then reiterates his confidence in the rock, in God, in whom alone
one can trust with confidence:

> For God alone my soul waits in silence,
>     for my hope is from him.
> He alone is my rock and my salvation,
>     my fortress; I shall not be shaken.
> On God rests my deliverance and my honor;
>     my mighty rock, my refuge is in God.

> Trust in him at all times, O people;
>> pour out your heart before him; God is a refuge for us.
>
> Those of low estate are but a breath,
>> those of high estate are a delusion;
> in the balances they go up;
>> they are together lighter than a breath.
> Put no confidence in extortion,
>> and set no vain hopes on robbery;
>> if riches increase, do not set your heart on them.
>
> Once God has spoken;
>> twice have I heard this:
> that power belongs to God,
>> and steadfast love belongs to you, O Lord. (vv. 5–12)

In two instances the metaphor of God as rock seems to be employed with a sense of irony. In both Psalms 28 and 31 the psalmist urges the rock to listen:

> To you, O Lord, I call;
>> my rock, do not refuse to hear me,
> for if you are silent to me,
>> I shall be like those who go down to the Pit. (28:1)

> Incline your ear to me;
>> rescue me speedily.
> Be a rock of refuge for me,
>> a strong fortress to save me. (31:2)

Can a rock hear? Of course not, and in these cases the psalmist may be employing the rock imagery as a part of his wrestling with his disorientation, his distance from God. These psalmists are in need, they are calling to God for help, but their experience may seem to imply that God does not hear any more than does a rock. The irony of these psalms is that God is the rock of refuge and protection, which is what the psalmist needs, but can the rock hear and be what the psalmist needs?

As with sleep, one must show a little care in reading the word "rock" and immediately equating it with God. The source domain retains its meaning in the psalms. Twice in Psalm 78 the rock is just a rock.

> He made streams come out of the rock,
>> and caused waters to flow down like rivers. . . .
> Even though he struck the rock
>> so that water gushed out and torrents overflowed,

can he also give bread,
>   or provide meat for his people? (vv. 16, 20)

But later in the same psalm, perhaps employing an intentional semantic tension with the earlier verse and playing on what was said before, the people are said to remember that

God was their rock,
>   the Most High God their redeemer. (v. 35)

Notice that the idea of God as "rock" is almost always associated with deliverance or salvation. The Rock is a place of safety and protection. There in the heights, behind unbreakable walls, the psalmist is preserved from his enemies. This is both how and who God is in these psalms.

We will note one final metaphor: God as warrior. Here again is a metaphor that will require us to engage our imaginations; some readers will need to work to suspend their initial reactions against such imagery. Psalm 24:8 answers the question "Who is the King of glory?" by describing God as a warrior:

The LORD, strong and mighty,
>   the LORD, mighty in battle.

Psalm 7 describes God's actions as a judge in the terms of a warrior, fighting on behalf of the psalmist:

God is my shield,
>   who saves the upright in heart.
God is a righteous judge,
>   and a God who has indignation every day.

If one does not repent, God will whet his sword;
>   he has bent and strung his bow;
he has prepared his deadly weapons,
>   making his arrows fiery shafts. (vv. 10–13)

God takes up the weapons of war in order to execute justice and judgment on Israel's behalf. Finally, in Psalm 44 the use of the metaphor is more subtle. Here the psalmist calls to mind God's actions on Israel's behalf in the past, the "deeds you performed in their days" (v. 1), in the vocabulary of the warrior. Deliverance has been effected through God's victories over Israel's enemies:

We have heard with our ears, O God,
>   our ancestors have told us,

what deeds you performed in their days,
    in the days of old:
you with your own hand drove out the nations,
    but them you planted;
you afflicted the peoples,
    but them you set free;
for not by their own sword did they win the land,
    nor did their own arm give them victory;
but your right hand, and your arm,
    and the light of your countenance,
    for you delighted in them.

You are my King and my God;
    you command victories for Jacob.
Through you we push down our foes;
    through your name we tread down our assailants.
For not in my bow do I trust,
    nor can my sword save me. (vv. 1–6)

Notice as well that this use of the metaphor is implicit; "God is a warrior" is never said explicitly, nor does the psalmist talk about God's strapping on the divine arsenal to go to war. Rather, the psalmist's own efforts in war are downplayed, and the source of Israel's victory is Israel's God.

The metaphor of God as fighting on behalf of Israel can be a difficult image for modern readers to know how to handle, but it is an important part of the theology of the psalms.[5] Israel's freedom, restoration, and faith are dependent on God the warrior. Biblical concepts of divine judgment, justice, and deliverance are inextricably tied to this image; indeed, the very identity of the people can be fully understood only when Yahweh God of the Heavenly Hosts is included in the picture the words of the psalm paint.

## Imagination and the Interpretation of the Psalms

Finish these sentences:

God is a(n) _____. God is like a(n) _____.

---

5. There is more than simply discomfort with the image of God as a warrior at stake here. As Richard Nysse puts it, "To excise this language from consideration in Old Testament theology would mean that the themes of liberation, creation, and hope would either be weakened or need to be drastically recast. Second, if God is to be part of a contemporary reappropriation of the Old Testament themes of liberation, creation, and ultimate hope, one needs to include Yahweh-is-a-Warrior. The Old Testament leaves little room for addressing such issues apart from talk about God." Nysse, "Yahweh Is a Warrior," *Word & World* 7, no. 2 (1987): 192–201, here 194.

Be creative. Come up with a metaphor from a modern source domain that the ancient Israelites would not have known. Maybe draw a metaphor from the engineering source domain of machines and engines. Or draw a metaphor from the electronic source domain of microprocessors or the internet. Or draw a metaphor from the source domain of atomic physics or modern chemistry.

What did you come up with?

Most people produce a positive, safe, friendly metaphor for God.

But this is not always the case in the psalms. As we have already shown, there is a need for interpretive imagination when reading metaphor in the psalms. This is especially true when we encounter metaphors that make us uncomfortable, such as the metaphor of God as warrior. There are other metaphors that we may experience as negative. One rather wild example brings the image of the divine warrior together with the idea of God's having had a few too many drinks. Psalm 78:65 describes God's rising to fight on Israel's behalf in a shocking scene:

> Then the Lord awoke as from sleep,
>     like a warrior shouting because of wine.

In this psalm we are to picture God as a drunken warrior who has passed out yet now awakens in a rage to battle on Israel's behalf.

That God is asleep in the first place is a striking image. Psalm 121:4 claims, "He who keeps Israel will neither slumber nor sleep." But several other psalms seem to suggest that God is doing just that! Two examples:

> Rouse yourself! Why do you sleep, O Lord?
>     Awake, do not cast us off forever! (44:23)

> Wake up! Bestir yourself for my defense,
>     for my cause, my God and my Lord! (35:23)

It is not entirely clear whether the psalmist really thinks that God is sleeping or if this is purely metaphorical. Certainly the perception of the psalmist may be taken as metaphorical. His experience is that God is not paying attention, that God is sleeping through his troubles. The image is employed to make sense of God's silence in the face of the psalmist's need.

Another example of a metaphor that might trouble modern readers is an image of how God punishes. Psalm 39 is a prayer for help, in which the psalmist's illness is consuming him. The psalm calls on God to forgive, to let the psalmist know what his end will be. He describes his physical suffering as a result of being consumed by God, like a moth consumes a threadbare garment:

> You chastise mortals
>> in punishment for sin,
> consuming like a moth what is dear to them;
>> surely everyone is a mere breath. (v. 11)

God the consuming moth! This is hardly the stuff of most church hymns or praise songs, but the image does convey rather effectively the sense the psalmist has of his wasting sickness and the part he believes God is playing in it.

## Ambiguity and the Extended Metaphor in the Psalms

Have you ever been confused by an image or a metaphor? Or perhaps more important, have you ever used a metaphor that someone else found confusing? For example, imagine a conversation between a dating couple. The young man says, "Cupcake, you mean the world to me." He meant it as a compliment and a confession of love. But she responds, "Did you just refer to me as a baked good that people serve at birthday parties? How gross and insensitive are you anyway?"

The truth is, sometimes metaphors are confusing, and their meaning can be less than totally clear.

The meaning of many metaphors seems obvious. But other metaphors are a little harder to identify; they are not quite so clearly recognized or interpreted. In this case, these subtle images may take more imagination to recognize and more care in their interpretation.

Confusion can happen for many reasons. One reason can be that a source domain that in one place and time had a very positive connotation may have developed a very negative connotation in another cultural time and place. For example, if we stray a bit outside the Psalter, the poetry in the book of Isaiah has an example of a metaphor that can be confusing. In Isaiah 25, the prophet is speaking to a people who were suffering, and he is intent on promising them that things will get better. He says,

> On this mountain the LORD of hosts will make for all peoples
>> a feast of rich food, a feast of well-aged wines,
> of rich food filled with marrow, of well-aged wines strained clear. (v. 6)

Many people cringe at the metaphor of eating a meal "filled with [bone] marrow." In ancient Israel, in which hunger and undernourishment were common and most people rarely ate meat, this image was very positive. Today, in an American culture in which obesity is common and in which many people

live at a great distance from the agricultural source of their food, the image
can repulse some people.

Similarly, Psalm 133 offers an ancient image of a community that is united
and not at odds:

> How good and pleasant it is
>     when God's people live together in unity!
> It is like precious oil poured on the head,
>     running down on the beard,
> running down on Aaron's beard,
>     down on the collar of his robe. (vv. 1–2 NIV)

In the ancient world, the image of anointing a guest with oil was a positive
image of hospitality and treating a guest right. But in the modern, Western
world, the image of pouring oil over a guest's head until the oil runs into
his beard and over his clothes—well, we will just say that some people find
this image confusing. And the point is that an engaged reader needs to do
a little digging to understand what the "source" of the image was trying to
communicate.

Another reason some metaphors are confusing is that there are some images in the psalms in which the source and target domains are relatively close.
As a result the makeup of the metaphor is somewhat ambiguous, demanding
greater imagination on the part of the interpreter. In Psalm 38, the psalmist's enemies—including his friends, companions, and neighbors—seem to
be standing aside from the psalmist and meditating on his state of affairs:

> My friends and companions stand aloof from my affliction,
>     and my neighbors stand far off.
>
> Those who seek my life lay their snares;
>     those who seek to hurt me speak of ruin,
>     and meditate treachery all day long.
>
> But I am like the deaf, I do not hear;
>     like the mute, who cannot speak.
> Truly, I am like one who does not hear,
>     and in whose mouth is no retort.
>
> But it is for you, O Lord, that I wait;
>     it is you, O Lord my God, who will answer. (vv. 11–15)

In the face of the enemy's murmuring, the psalmist neither listens to them
nor answers their attacks. The psalmist who is, one must assume, neither

deaf nor mute, presents himself as if he can neither hear the enemy's speech nor speak in his own defense. Instead, the psalmist waits for God to speak on his behalf. Here the source domain of the image is the physical realm of the human senses, and it appears to be applied to the same domain in finding its target. Is this, then, a metaphor? It is—though it is a metaphor that is more subtle than "The LORD is my shepherd." In Psalm 38 the metaphor of deafness and muteness is not related to the psalmist's physical state of being but to his reaction to his life situation. The psalmist waits for God patiently: because God is neither blind nor mute, God must see and answer.

In other psalms this same source domain—sight, hearing, speech—is employed to mock faith in idols:

> Their idols are silver and gold,
>   the work of human hands.
> They have mouths, but do not speak;
>   eyes, but do not see.
> They have ears, but do not hear;
>   noses, but do not smell.
> They have hands, but do not feel;
>   feet, but do not walk;
>   they make no sound in their throats.
> Those who make them are like them;
>   so are all who trust in them. (115:4–8; cf. 135:15–18)

The image of the idol is mocked by superimposing human attributes over an inanimate object. The metaphor compares the work of human hands and the attributes of human senses. By doing so, the metaphor creates a jarring image of something that is impossible.[6]

In other cases metaphor may appear to be a statement of reality but is actually a metaphor created through hyperbole. Consider Psalm 91:12–13:

> On their hands they [the angels] will bear you up,
>   so that you will not dash your foot against a stone.
> You will tread on the lion and the adder,
>   the young lion and the serpent you will trample under foot.

Are these claims for God's protection and provision to be taken literally? Perhaps. There are certainly some religious sects that take language like this quite literally. But it is also possible, and more likely, that Psalm 91 is best

---

6. Cf. Ps. 94:9, where the metaphor is reversed when applied to God: "He who planted the ear, does he not hear? He who formed the eye, does he not see?"

understood as a hyperbolic metaphor for the surety of one who says, "My refuge and my fortress; my God, in whom I trust" (v. 2).

Another somewhat ambiguous form of metaphor may at times be found in the poetic device called a merism (Greek: *merismos*). A merism is made up of two extremes, or two parts of something to represent the whole. "From east to west" means "everywhere"; "from head to toe" means "the whole body"; "from great to small" means "all people"; and so on. One merism of particular interest in the psalms is "the sun and the moon," which may refer to day and night or the constancy of something, usually God's protection. In one case this merism is employed as a blessing prayer for an enduring reign of the human king:

> May he live while the sun endures,
>     and as long as the moon, throughout all generations. (72:5)

In another psalm, sun and moon are employed to characterize enduring time and God's creative power in it:

> You have made the moon to mark the seasons;
>     the sun knows its time for setting. (104:19)

And again, sun and moon, as representative of all creation, are personified as praisers of God:

> Praise him, sun and moon;
>     praise him, all you shining stars! (148:3)

But in at least one case the sun-and-moon merism seems to function differently. In Psalm 121 the sun and the moon are presented as dangers, as threats to the psalmist, as "strikers" who may do the traveler harm:

> The sun shall not strike you by day,
>     nor the moon by night. (v. 6)

Sometimes a cigar is just a cigar, a rock is just a rock, and sometimes the moon is just the moon. But other times, well, the moon may have a different meaning. When it comes to Psalm 121, it is easy to understand that in a desert climate, people might be afraid of the sun's power to strike one down in the daytime. But what of the moon's striking at night? Scholars disagree about how to understand this reference. Some people think this is a reference to the superstitious view that the moon—especially the full moon—can have harmful effects. In this vein, James Limburg has written, "Exposure to moonlight was thought to cause mental disturbances; the word *lunatic*, from the Latin *luna*, 'moon,' still reflects this notion."[7] Other scholars have observed that Israel's neighbors worshiped the sun and moon as gods and have seen in this verse a reference to the sun and the moon as forces of darkness. Along this line of thought, Hans-Joachim Kraus has written, "In the Babylonian world disastrous effects are ascribed to the moon-god. Fever and leprosy are caused by him. But the thought can also be about the affliction of being moonstruck, which was understood to be possession by demons, . . . [and against such threats the psalm promises that] Yahweh 'watches' and 'protects.'"[8] But the majority of scholars simply view the "sun and moon" as a merism indicating that God protects all the time. Craig Broyles can speak for this majority approach: "The parallel expressions of the sun and the moon do not signify distinct entities (as though we should strain to discover how the moon itself could harm us) but rather the totality of day and night."[9]

The point we are making here is that the precise meaning of some metaphors is ambiguous—there is a range of possible answers. But in spite of ambiguity about the precise meaning of the metaphor, there is still agreement about the general, promissory meaning of the passage. The metaphor of God as the "shade" that protects a traveler from the sun and the moon is a promise of God's protective power extending over and shielding the traveler from danger.

## Conclusion

Metaphor is fundamental to the poetic nature of the psalms. The poetry of the psalms creates meaning by painting word pictures through which the reader can make sense of life, develop a robust theological imagination, and connect not only to the ancient world out of which the psalms arose but also make sense of the present world in which the psalm reader now lives. The metaphors employed in the Hebrew Bible are a mix of the familiar and the discomforting. Is God a shepherd, a rock, or a light? Or is God a consuming moth, a sound sleeper, or a drunken warrior? In the collected metaphors of the psalms, the answer is yes. Metaphor both requires and empowers imagination in interpretation, which makes reading the psalms both a challenge and a joy.

7. James Limburg, *Psalms* (Louisville: Westminster John Knox, 2000), 424.

8. Hans-Joachim Kraus, *Psalms 60–150*, trans. Hilton C. Oswald (trans. of 5th German ed., 1978; Minneapolis: Augsburg, 1989), 430.

9. Craig Broyles, *Psalms* (Peabody, MA: Hendrickson, 1999), 449.

## PSALM 23 IN CONTEMPORARY MUSIC

As other sidebars have highlighted, the use of Psalm 23 in popular culture mirrors its familiarity. Psalm 23 is the most recognizable psalm, and it is also the most widely used in popular culture. Frequently in music the metaphors of Psalm 23 are reimagined. Consider how the image of "the valley of the shadow of death" is appropriated in songs like these:

Coolio's "Gangsta's Paradise":

> *As I walk through the valley of the shadow of death*
> I take a look at my life and realize there's nothing left

Kanye West's "Jesus Walks":

> *I walk through the valley of the Chi where death is*
> Top floor the view alone will leave you breathless Uhhhh!

Good Charlotte's "The River":

> *As I walk through the valley of the shadow of LA*
> The footsteps that were next to me have gone their separate ways

There are, as well, others, from Megadeth's heavy-metal dirge "Shadow of Deth," in which a strangely gothic version of the Psalm 23 is spoken (in a fake English accent), to the borrowing of Psalm 23:4 in U2's "Love Rescue Me."

## GOING DEEPER

To deepen your grasp of the concepts introduced in this chapter, consider doing one or more of the following exercises:

1. Make a list of five to ten metaphors that describe who you are as a person. Next, make a list of five to ten metaphors for God. Are there similarities between the two lists? Differences? What are they, and how does making such lists help you think both theologically about God and about yourself?

2. Open a Bible to Psalm 23. Rewrite Psalm 23:1–4, replacing the shepherd metaphor with a metaphor from your own daily living. What kind of image of how God is in relationship with human beings makes the most sense to you?

3. Ask a friend or friends to think up three metaphors for God. Metaphors are both true and not true at the same time (God is both like a rock in some ways [strong, reliable] and not like a rock in some ways [mute, unthinking]). How is God both *like* the metaphor your friend or friends thought of and *not like* that metaphor?

## FOR FURTHER READING

Brown, William P. *Seeing the Psalms: A Theology of Metaphor*. Louisville: Westminster John Knox, 2002.

Hecke, Pierre van, ed. *Metaphor in the Hebrew Bible*. Dudley, MA: Peeters, 2005.

Keel, Othmar. *The Symbolism of the Biblical World: Ancient Near Eastern Iconography and the Book of Psalms*. Winona Lake, IN: Eisenbrauns, 1997.

# Why Are the Psalms
# in This Order?

*Learning to Interpret Psalms*
*within the Context of the Book of Psalms*

## Introducing the Shape and Shaping of the Psalter
## ("Canonical Interpretation")

In most Christian and Jewish Bibles, the book of Psalms consists of 150 psalms.[1] The sequence of these 150 psalms (including the division between individual poems) became fixed over time. Interpreters who are interested in the "shape and shaping of the Psalter" seek to understand what a psalm means in its particular place within the book of Psalms.

Recall that at the start of chapter 2 readers were invited to reflect on the importance of *context* when interpreting words and sentences. In what we hope was a lighthearted manner, we compared how the words "Clean Bathrooms!!!" might mean two completely different things in two different contexts. On the one hand, if they were handwritten and taped to your door on a "to-do list," they would be a command: *Remember to clean the bathrooms.*

---

1. Some Orthodox and even Catholic Bibles include an additional poem, Ps. 151. This poem is included in the Septuagint, the ancient Greek translation of the Hebrew Bible.

On the other hand, if they were professionally printed and posted in a gas station window, they would be a promise: *If you buy your gas here, we've got clean bathrooms you can use.*

For scholars who are interested in canonical interpretation of the Psalter, there are two main issues. The first issue is that the context in which psalms are to be read is the Psalter itself. The second issue is that the Psalter as a whole has a meaning; it isn't just a collection of 150 poems that each have meaning. The Psalter itself is like a mosaic. Each of the psalms is a small stone with individual meaning, but seen together, they have a composite meaning.

In terms of the meaning of the individual psalms, the context of the Psalter is the only "real" context that exists.

For most of the twentieth century, the majority of interpreters of the psalms would read a psalm and then imagine the "historical context" in which the psalm may have been written or performed in the ancient world. For example, consider the praise hymn Psalm 100, which begins, "Shout to the Lord, all the earth. Worship the Lord with joy; come into his presence with joyful shouts" (vv. 1–2 AT). An interpreter might imagine the context in which the psalm was sung at a festival worship service in the temple in Jerusalem, or, conversely, a clan worship service in a small town. Another example is the royal hymn Psalm 2, which speaks of "the Lord" and "his anointed one" (v. 2 AT) and in which God says, "I have set my king on Zion, my holy mountain" (v. 6 AT). Many interpreters imagine that this psalm was written for and performed at the coronation of a Davidic king in Jerusalem and interpret its meaning within that reconstructed historical context.

In 1985, Gerald Wilson published a groundbreaking book titled *The Editing of the Hebrew Psalter.*[2] In it, Wilson applied the assumptions and principles of canonical criticism (which had already been productively applied to many other books of the Bible) to the book of Psalms. One of the principles of this approach to interpretation is that while it is often helpful to imagine ancient life settings as the contexts in which individual psalms can be interpreted, all of these imagined contexts are only that, imagined. We can never be certain about these reconstructed contexts; at the very best, they can be viewed only as probable or likely. And in many or most cases, these reconstructed contexts can never be better than improbable or unlikely.

But there is one context that doesn't need to be imagined at all: the context of the book of Psalms. The only context we have that is absolutely certain for each psalm is the Psalter itself. Psalm 2 comes after Psalm 1 and before Psalm 3. What might Psalm 2 mean in that very concrete setting?

---

2. Gerald H. Wilson, *The Editing of the Hebrew Psalter* (Chico, CA: Scholars Press, 1985).

Psalm 100 comes in the middle of Book IV of the Psalter, after Psalms 90–99 and before Psalms 101–106. What might Psalm 100 mean in that very concrete context?

This makes sense as far as that goes. But as the great football commentator Lee Corso would say, "Not so fast, my friend!" The Psalter itself must be interpreted within a context. And when it comes to the context in which the Psalter was edited and shaped, there are more clear questions than there are clear answers.

When was the Psalter edited and when did it take its final shape? Who edited the Psalter and when? Was it one group editing during one time period? Was it multiple groups editing in multiple stages over many years? Did this editing happen in one location or in more than one location? What were the historical events that influenced the editors? What theological convictions and commitments informed their work? In order to understand the meaning of the book of Psalms, these questions (and more) need answers. And, as is inevitably the case in biblical studies, different scholars answer these questions differently. Here are some examples:

- Gerald Wilson argued that the final edition of the Psalter did not occur until the end of the first century CE (fifty to seventy years after Jesus).
- The German scholars Frank-Lothar Hossfeld and Erich Zenger argued that the final edition occurred in the second century BCE and that there were multiple layers of editing, which they feel confident of being able to reconstruct.
- The British scholar Susan Gillingham prefers an earlier date for the final edition and has argued that a group of Levitical temple musicians were responsible for it.
- The American scholar Dennis Tucker has suggested a date late in what is known as the Persian Period, when Judah was a province in the Persian Empire, so perhaps sometime after 400 BCE. Another German scholar, Matthias Millard, also argues for a date in the Persian Period (ca. 540–333 BCE).[3]

---

3. Gerald H. Wilson, "A First-Century C.E. Date for the Closing of the Psalter?," in *Haim M. I. Gevaryahu: Memorial Volume*, ed. Joshua J. Adler (Jerusalem: World Jewish Bible Center, 1990), 136–43; Frank-Lothar Hossfeld and Erich Zenger, *Die Psalmen I: Psalm 1–50* (Würzburg: Echter, 1993); Susan Gillingham, "The Zion Tradition and the Editing of the Hebrew Psalter," in *Temple and Worship in Biblical Israel*, ed. John Day (London: T&T Clark, 2005), 308–41; also Gillingham's magisterial *Psalms through the Centuries*, 3 vols. (Oxford: Blackwell, 2008; Hoboken, NJ: Wiley Blackwell, 2018–22); and W. Dennis Tucker Jr.,

The point is that when it comes to understanding the "historical context" in which the Psalter as a whole reached final form, there is no agreement, and thus there is no fixed context in which to interpret the book of Psalms. And this means that even when asking a question such as "What does Psalm 2 mean in the context of the Psalter?" different interpreters will arrive at different interpretations of a psalm's meaning. And of course that goes for the meaning of the Psalter as a whole. If one follows Wilson and concludes that the final shape was fixed toward the end of the first century, then one might imagine that the book of Psalms' final form shows a response to the destruction of Jerusalem around 70 CE by the Romans (or perhaps even to the proclamation that Jesus is the Messiah). If, on the other hand, one follows Millard and Tucker, who imagine that the final form took shape as much as four hundred to five hundred years earlier, then one might imagine that the Psalter's final shape is a response to the end of the Babylonian exile and the rise of the Persian Empire.

But none of this is to say that the whole enterprise is pointless; it is not. As we will see, canonical interpretation of the Psalter nevertheless offers productive insights. Before describing these major insights, however, it will be helpful to describe the basic shape of the Psalter and essential realities concerning the Psalter that most scholars agree on.

## The Shape and Shaping of the Hebrew Psalter: The Basics

When it comes to the shape and shaping of the Hebrew Psalter, there are some basic, agreed-on realities that few doubt.

### The Superscriptions and Other "Paratextual" Markers Are Important Clues

The text of the book of Psalms includes not only the words of the psalms themselves but also what scholars call "paratextual" elements—words, titles, and verses added to the psalms by later editors and collectors. Even when the meaning of certain terms is no longer clear, the existence of these terms can still offer clues in regard to the editing process. These paratextual elements are important clues as to the development of the Psalter, and they include the following:

---

*Constructing and Deconstructing Power in Psalms 107–150* (Atlanta: SBL Press, 2014); Matthias Millard, *Die Komposition des Psalters: Ein Formgeschichtlicher Ansatz* (Tübingen: Mohr, 1994).

- The superscriptions, which include the following:
  - Titles of the subcollections to which psalms belong, such as "of David," "of the sons of Korah," "of Asaph," "a song of ascents," "to the leader"
  - Notes on performance whose meaning is largely lost, such as "with stringed instruments," "for the flutes," "according to the *Sheminith*"
  - Historical notes, such as "of David, when he fled from his son Absalom" (Ps. 3) and "when the prophet Nathan approached him, after he had gone in to Bathsheba" (Ps. 51 AT)
  - Names of song genre, such as "a *Shiggaion*," "a psalm," "praise," "a *Maskil*," "a prayer"
  - Notes on the use of certain psalms, such as "A song at the dedication of the temple," "a song for the Sabbath Day," "a prayer of one afflicted, when faint and pleading before the LORD," "for instruction," "for thanksgiving," "for the memorial offering"
- The four doxologies, which were added and divide the Psalter into five books (41:13; 72:18–19; 89:52; 106:48)
- The one explicit editorial note in the Psalter: "The prayers of David son of Jesse are come to an end" (72:20 AT)
- The indecipherable marker *Selah*, which occurs seventy-one times in thirty-nine psalms (and three times in the preexilic book of Habakkuk)

### Subcollections within the Psalter

One of the most obvious, but often unnoted, aspects of the shape and shaping of the Psalter is that it is *a collection of subcollections*. The Psalter clearly came into existence gradually, as individual psalms were collected into subcollections and as those subcollections were joined together over time. Although some scholars believe that it is possible to reconstruct to a remarkable degree the process via which the Psalter slowly grew, we do not believe that anyone can reconstruct this process with any degree of detail or confidence. However, we do believe that a few fairly broad conclusions seem plausible.

First, many of the subcollections from which the Psalter was formed can be identified with a high degree of confidence. These can be identified by titles in the superscriptions, or by the internal content of the psalms, or by later liturgical use. These subcollections include the following:

- The major Davidic collection(s) (3–41; 51–72)
  - □ "The prayers of David the son of Jesse are ended" (72:20)
- The smaller Davidic collections (108–110; 138–145)
- The psalms of Asaph (50; 73–83)
- The psalms of the Korahites (42/43–49; 84–85; 87–88)
- The Psalms of Ascent (120–134)
- The Elohistic Psalter (42–83)
- The enthronement psalms (93–99)
- The Egyptian Hallel (113–118)
- The twin psalms (103–104; 105–106; 111–112)

It may be that not all of these were separate subcollections prior to being incorporated into the Psalter. Some, such as the psalms of David, of Asaph, of the Korahites, and the enthronement psalms, seem to have been separate collections that were incorporated into a growing Psalter. Others, such as the twin psalms, the Egyptian Hallel, and the Psalms of Ascent, may represent the activity of editors who placed these psalms together in the Psalter.

It is interesting to note that with the exception of Psalm 50, the psalms of Asaph were incorporated as one unit (Pss. 73–83). The psalms of the Korahites, on the other hand, were separated into three units. Most psalms scholars conclude that the psalms of Asaph and the psalms of the Korahites originated in places different from those of the psalms of David and other later psalms.

### From Front to Back (Broadly Speaking)

In general, we can conclude that the Psalter grew from front to back, with the earlier sections taking shape prior to the latter sections. This development can be traced in a few ways, the most important of which is through noting earlier versus later linguistic forms. On the one hand, earlier-occurring psalms, such as Psalm 2, contain more ancient linguistic features, such as old words and *olde wayes* of spelling. On the other hand, later-occurring psalms, such as the Psalms of Ascent (Pss. 120–134), contain later linguistic features and words and #*modernways* of spelling. (These differences in spelling and words are evident only in the Hebrew; English translations obscure this.) This conclusion is also supported by several other details. The psalms of David predominate in the first two books of the Psalter, with other, younger subcollections coming after. Psalm 19:1–6 and Psalm 29 are widely thought to be very old, perhaps even being pre-Israelite hymns that were edited and adapted to Israel's God. The fact that the vast majority of the occurrences of indecipherable terms such as *Shiggaion*, *Sheminith*, *Gittith*, and *Selah* occur in Psalms 3–89 *may* also suggest that these psalms tend to be older.

### Other Basic Aspects of the Shaping of the Psalter

The psalms did not all originate in the same place or time. For example, Psalms 2 and 46 both assume a Jerusalem location, most probably prior to the exile in 586 BCE, whereas Psalms 137 and 120, by comparison, seem to assume non-Jerusalem locations in exile, thus probably after 586 BCE. As various subcollections were compiled, some psalms were joined together, inserted between subcollections, or dropped altogether. The various subcollections most likely did not all have the same functions. Some may have been intended for use in public worship, but others may have been intended for more intimate prayer or ritual uses.

Gerald Wilson argued that two major subcollections, Psalms 2–72 and Psalms 73–89, have two different editorial histories and two different meanings:

> The combined collection of Pss 2–72 might represent a pre-exilic collection reflecting more positively and hopefully on the fortunes of the Davidic kingship, while the extension in 73–89 modifies these hopes in light of the exilic experience. . . .
> . . . The thematic development revealed in the placement of these psalms at the "seams" of the first three books agrees with the evaluation above. In its final form it reflects exilic (or post-exilic) evaluation of the hopes of the Davidic monarchy based on the covenant of David. The conclusion still manifests hope in the faithfulness of YHWH to his covenant promises and a plea for restoration.[4]

Another agreed-on observation about the shape of the Psalter is that the Psalter ends with praise: Psalms 146–150 are all praise hymns that begin and end with the exclamation, "Praise the LORD!" (*halelu-yah* in Hebrew). Some regard these five hymns as a whole as the final doxology of the book of Psalms. Others regard only Psalm 150 as the closing doxology.

Three conclusions regarding the editorial shape of the Psalter enjoy widespread acceptance: (1) Psalms 1–2 provide a two-part introduction to the Psalter; (2) royal and wisdom psalms have been placed at the "seams" between the books of the Psalter; (3) there is a major editorial shift in the Psalter between Books I–III (Pss. 1–89) and Books IV–V (Pss. 90–150).

---

4. Gerald Wilson, "The Use of Royal Psalms at the Seams of the Hebrew Psalter," *Journal for the Study of the Old Testament* 35 (1986): 91–92.

### The Two-Part Introduction to the Psalter: Psalms 1 and 2

Psalms 1 and 2 were placed at the start of the Psalter in order to provide a two-poem introduction to the Psalter. Psalm 1 is a wisdom (instructional) psalm. It promises that those who "delight in the *Torah* of the LORD" will be "like a tree transplanted by streams of water" (vv. 2–3 AT). Such a person will be strong, will bear fruit in its season, and will prosper in adversity. Psalm 2 is a royal psalm and recalls the Lord's promise to King David's descendants: "I have set my king on Zion, my holy mountain" (v. 6 AT).

This two-part introduction has been interpreted in various ways by scholars. At the least, it (1) introduces the Psalter itself as Scripture that is to be meditated on and as instruction in following God, and (2) introduces the Psalter as a book of messianic promise about God's work through the Davidic monarchy and God's coming work through the Messiah. William Brown has

---

## MORNING AND EVENING IN PSALMS 3–6

After Psalms 1–2, which form the two-part introduction to the Psalter, the next four psalms follow a morning-evening-morning-evening pattern.

> Psalm 3: "I lie down and I sleep; I awake, for the LORD sustains me" (v. 5 AT).
>
> Psalm 4: "When you are anxious, do not sin; speak to your hearts upon your beds and be still"; "I both lie down and I sleep in peace; for you alone, LORD, make me dwell in safety" (vv. 4, 8 AT).
>
> Psalm 5: "O LORD, in the morning you hear my voice; in the morning I lay out before you, and watch" (v. 3 AT).
>
> Psalm 6: "I grow weary with my sighing; every night I swim in my bed; I melt my couch with my weeping" (v. 6 AT).

Susan Gillingham has further identified morning and evening themes in Psalms 7 and 8:

> Psalm 7: "Rise up!" and "Awake!" the psalmist urges God (v. 6 AT).
>
> Psalm 8: "When I look at the heavens—the work of your fingers—the moon and stars, which you have made firm . . ." (v. 3 AT).[a]

Imagine praying these six psalms over three days—morning and evening. How would these psalms come to mean something different as a sequence than if read individually?

a. Susan Gillingham, *Psalms through the Centuries* (Oxford: Blackwell, 2008; Hoboken, NJ: Wiley Blackwell, 2018–22), 2:68–73.

invited readers of the Psalter to trace "the themes featured in these introductory psalms through the entire" Psalter.[5]

### Royal and Wisdom Psalms at the Seams

The Psalter has been editorially divided into five books. This editorial division itself is significant because it is an invitation to read the psalms as Scripture. Just as there are five books in the Pentateuch, so also there are five books in the Psalter. But it is perhaps even more important to note that royal and wisdom psalms were placed at the "seams" between certain books of the Psalter. Gerald Wilson demonstrated that certain royal psalms, most notably Psalms 2; 72; and 89, were intentionally inserted at the seams of the Psalter.[6] The same can be seen with wisdom psalms.

- Book I (1–41)
  □ Ps. 1, wisdom; Ps. 2, royal
  □ Ps. 41, wisdom
- Book II (42–72)
  □ Ps. 72, royal
- Book III (73–89)
  □ Ps. 73, wisdom
  □ Ps. 89, royal
- Book IV (90–106)
  □ Ps. 90, wisdom
- Book V (107–150)

One thing to note is that the presence of the wisdom and royal psalms at the seams of the Psalter stops abruptly with the transition from Book III to Book IV (more on this next). Most likely this change indicates that there were different stages of editing the Psalter and that different editorial techniques were used by editors in Books I–III of the Psalter (Pss. 1–89) as compared to Books IV–V (Pss. 90–150).

The question is, however, What does this mean? As asserted earlier in this chapter, the most obvious conclusion is that the presence of the wisdom (instructional) psalms at the seams of the Psalter means that the editors were signaling that the psalms are to be read as instruction in the spiritual

5. William P. Brown, *Psalms*, Interpreting Biblical Texts (Nashville: Abingdon, 2010), 112–13.
6. Wilson, "Use of Royal Psalms."

life. These words and prayers are given for those who follow God to pray, to sing, to study, and to meditate on. (And this is exactly how the psalms were read in the New Testament, in Judaism, and in Christianity.) The presence of the royal psalms—long after there had ceased to be kings in Israel and Judah—meant that the Psalter was to be read and interpreted as a book of messianic promise. (And this is also how the psalms were read in the New Testament and in other first-century Jewish communities such as the community at Qumran.)

### The "Break" between Psalms 1–89 and 90–150 (between Book III and Book IV)

As is already indicated above, the major editorial shift in the Psalter comes with the transition from Book III (which culminates with Ps. 89) to Book IV (which begins with Ps. 90). The German scholar Frank-Lothar Hossfeld in many places referred to this transition as the major *caesura* in the book of Psalms—the most important break or interruption.

*Psalm 89.* Psalm 89 concludes the second Davidic Psalter, which has such a great focus on the voice and person of King David. It is important to know that in 2 Samuel 7, the Lord had made a covenant with David. In that covenant, the Lord promised David the following:

> When your days are fulfilled and you lie down with your forefathers, I will raise up your offspring [Hebrew: "seed"] after you, who shall come from your body, and I will establish his kingdom. He shall build a house [temple] for my name, and I will establish the throne of his kingdom forever. I will be father to him, and he shall be son to me. When he sins, I will punish him with a rod such as humans use, with blows inflicted by human beings. But I will not take my steadfast love from him, as I took it from Saul, whom I put away from before you. Your house [dynasty] and your kingdom shall be made sure forever before me; your throne shall be established forever. (2 Sam. 7:12–16 AT)

Psalm 89 is a royal psalm with three parts. In the first part of the psalm (vv. 1–18), the psalm celebrates the Lord as creator and ruler of all:

> <sup>6</sup> For who in the skies above can compare with the LORD?
>     Who is like the LORD among the heavenly beings?
> <sup>7</sup> In the council of the holy ones God is greatly feared;
>     he is more awesome than all who surround him.
> <sup>8</sup> Who is like you, LORD God Almighty?
>     You, LORD, are mighty, and your faithfulness surrounds you.

⁹ You rule over the surging sea;
  when its waves mount up, you still them.
¹⁰ You crushed Rahab like one of the slain;
  with your strong arm you scattered your enemies.
¹¹ The heavens are yours, and yours also the earth;
  you founded the world and all that is in it. (vv. 6–11 NIV)

The poem emphasizes the Lord's universal power and reign both in heaven ("Who is like the LORD among the heavenly beings?") and on earth ("With your strong arm you scattered your enemies").

In the second part of the psalm (vv. 19–37), the poet celebrates the covenant that the Lord made with David:

²⁰ I have found David my servant;
  with my sacred oil I have anointed him.
²¹ My hand will sustain him;
  surely my arm will strengthen him.
²² The enemy will not get the better of him;
  the wicked will not oppress him.
²³ I will crush his foes before him
  and strike down his adversaries. . . .
²⁸ I will maintain my love to him forever,
  and my covenant with him will never fail.
²⁹ I will establish his line forever,
  his throne as long as the heavens endure.

³⁰ If his sons forsake my law
  and do not follow my statutes,
³¹ if they violate my decrees
  and fail to keep my commands,
³² I will punish their sin with the rod,
  their iniquity with flogging;
³³ but I will not take my love from him,
  nor will I ever betray my faithfulness.
³⁴ I will not violate my covenant
  or alter what my lips have uttered. (vv. 20–23, 28–34 NIV)

The rhetoric of the psalm asserts that the creator of all has promised to exercise the divine power in order to protect David's descendants and ensure their perpetual reign.

But in the third part of the psalm (vv. 38–51), the poet laments the fall of the Davidic monarchy, most likely referring to the destruction of Jerusalem in 586 BCE at the hands of the Babylonians (although this is not specifically named). The language that the psalm uses is shocking; it may be the most visceral lament and direct challenge to God in the entire Psalter:

> [38] But you have rejected, you have spurned,
>       you have been very angry with your anointed one.
> [39] You have renounced the covenant with your servant
>       and have defiled his crown in the dust.
> [40] You have broken through all his walls
>       and reduced his strongholds to ruins. (vv. 38–40 NIV)

The verbs are shocking, scandalous: "You have rejected, you have spurned . . ." and "You have renounced the covenant with your servant." The "servant" refers not to David, who is long dead, but to his descendant (his "son" [see v. 30]) who was on the throne at the time of the national defeat, presumably King Jehoiachin or King Zedekiah, the last of Judah's reigning kings. The psalm reminds the Lord of the divine promises that had been made to David, "I will not violate [Hebrew: *ḥalal*] my covenant," but it then accuses God of having done exactly that: "You have . . . violated [Hebrew: *ḥalal*] his crown in the dust" (v. 39 AT). The psalm then intensifies the lament by asking typical lament questions to which there is no apparent answer and making a final plea in verse 50, "Remember, Lord, . . . your servant" (presumably the deposed king):

> [46] How long, LORD? Will you hide yourself forever?
>       How long will your wrath burn like fire?
> [47] Remember how fleeting is my life.
>       For what futility you have created all humanity!
> [48] Who can live and not see death,
>       or who can escape the power of the grave?
> [49] Lord, where is your former great love,
>       which in your faithfulness you swore to David?
> [50] Remember, Lord, how your servant has been mocked,
>       how I bear in my heart the taunts of all the nations,
> [51] the taunts with which your enemies, LORD, have mocked,
>       with which they have mocked every step of your anointed one.
>          (vv. 46–51 NIV)

The doxology that follows and that culminates Book III, "Praise be to the LORD forever! Amen and Amen," is the weakest and briefest of the four editorial doxologies (v. 52 NIV). And for good reason: the royal Psalm 89 ends in lament. The Davidic covenant seems to have failed. Gerald Wilson writes, "The Davidic covenant introduced in Ps 2 has come to nothing and the combination of three books concludes with the anguished cry of the Davidic descendants."[7]

*Psalm 90.* Those who study the editorial shape of the Psalter note that Psalm 90, the first psalm in Book IV, "answers" the questions and laments of the royal Psalm 89. It is a wisdom psalm, and its superscription describes it as "a prayer of Moses, the man of God" (AT). This is the only psalm of Moses in the Psalter. Moses was, of course, the one whom God used to lead the people out of Egypt, through the wilderness, and into the land. He was the "man of God" before there were any kings—long before David. The closing lines of the book of Deuteronomy state, "There has not arisen a prophet in Israel like Moses, whom the LORD knew face-to-face" (34:10 AT). Does Psalm 90 "answer" Psalm 89 by replacing David and human kingship in Israel with Moses and obedience to the law—a Torah piety? Some interpreters have argued so.

*Psalms 93–100.* As Book IV of the Psalter continues, the next group of psalms that one encounters are known as the enthronement psalms (Pss. 93; 95–99). All of these psalms are hymns that contain a Hebrew phrase that is translated as either "The LORD reigns!" or "The LORD has become king!" or "The LORD is king!" If one reads this group of psalms as the "answer" to the questions and crisis of Psalm 89, does this suggest that the Psalter's "answer" to failed human kingship is the proclamation "The LORD is king"? Some interpreters have argued so.

The above are a sampling of what we regard as the most important and widely acknowledged editorial features of the shape and shaping of the Psalter. We have also hinted at the range of interpretations of what this shape might mean.

## Interpreting the Meaning of the Psalter as a Whole

As has been noted, there are a range of interpretations of what the Psalter as a whole might mean. There are also a range of methods of interpreting the meaning of the Psalter. Some interpreters employ very historically oriented methods of various types. The German scholars Frank-Lothar Hossfeld and Erich Zenger (and their students), for example, believed that they could reconstruct with a high degree of plausibility the various phases through which the Psalter grew over the centuries. Having built that reconstruction, they then interpreted the meaning of these various editorial phases. For example, they believed that the following stages of editorial growth were discernible:

---

7. Wilson, *Editing of the Hebrew Psalter*, 213.

- "At the beginning of the fifth century [B.C.E.] a Psalter beginning with Psalm 2 concluded with Psalm 100 and the whole composition can be called the 'YHWH is king Psalter.'"
- "In the middle of the fifth century B.C.E.," Psalms 101–106 may have been added; this new Psalter they then call "the historical-theological Psalter."
- Another editorial "was created around 400 B.C.E. by (Levitical) Temple singers through the addition of Psalms 107–136 (sometimes using existing individual psalms or groups of psalms)."
- The addition of a fifth Davidic Psalter (Pss. 138–145) "reveals characteristics of wisdom and Priestly language and concepts, here appearing in a synthesis of wisdom and Priestly thought in connection with a value system of universal space and restricted time. The suggested dating is at the end of the Persian period, therefore near the close of the fourth century B.C.E."
- Later, Psalms 1, 2:10–12, and 137 were added: a "Torah Psalter."
- Finally, Psalms 146–150 and 86 were added, changing the Torah Psalter into the final "Book of Praises." "We can imagine this redaction taking place between 200 and 150 B.C.E., in the context of the struggle against the Seleucids, but it could have been completed as early as the third century."[8]

Gerald Wilson also worked from a historical perspective, but he focused mostly on the final form of text, without believing that he could reconstruct the complicated history of the growth of the Psalter.

Other scholars have preferred a literary method, focusing simply on the final form of the Psalter as a literary document. These scholars have included prominent people such as Nancy deClaissé-Walford and Walter Brueggemann.

Since 1985, there have literally been hundreds and hundreds of books, essays, and articles written concerning the shape and shaping of the Psalter. The best summaries of this growing corpus of work are those by David Howard (with Michael Snearly), Kenneth Kuntz, and Beat Weber.[9]

David Howard and Michael Snearly have performed the wonderful service of summarizing two main ways that scholars have interpreted the meaning

---

8. Frank-Lothar Hossfeld and Erich Zenger, *Psalms 3: A Commentary on Psalms 101–150*, trans. Linda M. Maloney, ed. Klaus Baltzer (Minneapolis: Fortress, 2011), 1–7.

9. See the bibliographical references on page 1 in David M. Howard Jr. and Michael K. Snearly, "Reading the Psalter as a Unified Book: Recent Trends," in *Reading the Psalms Theologically*, ed. David M. Howard Jr. and Andrew J. Schmutzer (Bellingham, WA: Lexham Academic, 2023): 1–35.

of the Psalter as a book. They start by recognizing Gerald Wilson's ground-breaking work. Noting the major break between Psalms 1–89 and 90–150, they summarize Wilson's original conclusion as follows: "For Wilson and most who have followed him . . . Psalm 89 is pivotal in that here the Davidic covenant is viewed as 'broken, failed.' The rest of the Psalter attempts to deal with this 'failure,' focusing on Yahweh's (not David's) eternal kingship and the importance of Torah obedience. Wilson saw a 'final wisdom frame' that 'had the last word' over an earlier 'royal covenant frame' that had emphasized the (failed) Davidic covenant."[10] Many scholars have since agreed with Wilson's main conclusion, but others have offered a second interpretation. Howard and Snearly helpfully trace what they see as the two main ways in which the shape of the Psalter has been construed, which we will now look at briefly.

### "Wisdom/Democratizing Approaches"

Howard and Snearly state,

Following Wilson's lead, many scholars argue that all the roles, actions, and functions attributed to the royal figure in the Psalms ultimately are applied to the people of God at large. God's kingdom will be ushered in by his people, not by a single, specific person (Messiah). Such a wisdom or democratizing perspective is signaled at the outset by the wisdom in Psalm 1 and at the end by the kingship of Yahweh in Psalm 145. The "David" found in the latter parts of the Psalter (especially Pss 138–144) is seen as weak, dependent on Yahweh the Great King, and his future is nonexistent or else absorbed into Yahweh's kingship.[11]

### "Royal/Messianic Approaches"

Howard and Snearly write, "The other main trajectory of editorial-critical analysis sees David—and, by extension, the anointed Davidic king—as the central figure, along with Yahweh himself, of the book from beginning to end."[12] They cite the work of David Mitchell, who argued that the Psalter should be read as a book of messianic promise (which, incidentally, is how both the New Testament and Qumran interpreted the Psalter). They quote Mitchell's argument that the Psalter "was designed by its redactors as a purposefully ordered arrangement of lyrics with an eschatological message. This message . . . consists of a predicted sequence of eschatological events. These include Israel in exile, the appearing of a messianic superhero, the ingathering

10. Howard and Snearly, "Reading the Psalter," 4–5.
11. Howard and Snearly, "Reading the Psalter," 5–6.
12. Howard and Snearly, "Reading the Psalter," 11.

of Israel, the attack of the nations, the hero's suffering, the scattering of Israel in the wilderness, their ingathering and further imperilment, the appearance of a superhero from the heavens to rescue them, the establishment of his *malkut* [kingship] from Zion, the prosperity of Israel and the homage of the nations."[13]

### Criticisms of Shape and Shaping

In recent years, some scholars have begun pushing back on the entire notion of reading the Psalter as a book. The most prominent of these have been Norman Whybray, Erhard Gerstenberger, and David Davage (neé Willgren).[14] Gerstenberger prefers to understand the Psalter as a "hymnbook"—precisely the concept that Wilson, Hossfeld, and Zenger had rejected. Davage prefers the concept of the Psalter as a "garden" in which individual flowers (psalms) are collected for use: "Like a garden of flowers, the 'Book' of Psalms does not primarily provide a literary context for individual psalms, but rather preserves a dynamic selection of psalms that had proven to stand the test of time and ultimately had come to be regarded, not only as words *to* God, but as words through which God's voice could be heard."[15]

## Reading Individual Psalms in the Literary Context of the Psalter

In spite of David Davage's and Erhard Gerstenberger's well-argued pushback on the broader enterprise of interpreting the meaning of the Psalter as a whole, we think that there is evidence that at least some ancient interpreters of the psalms did use and interpret at least some psalms in sequence. The Egyptian Hallel, for instance, is Psalms 113–118. In Judaism, this sequence of psalms was (and is) sung at Passover. Psalms 113–114 are sung before the Passover meal and Psalms 115–118 are sung after. And it is logical to conclude that if sung together, they would be interpreted as a sequence. Likewise, the three sets of twin psalms (Pss. 103–104; 105–106; 111–112) are clearly arranged to be read/sung and interpreted as pairs.

13. Howard and Snearly, "Reading the Psalter," 11, quoting David Mitchell, *The Message of the Psalter: An Eschatological Programme in the Book of Psalms* (Sheffield: Sheffield Academic, 1997), 15.
14. Norman Whybray, *Reading the Psalms as a Book* (Sheffield: Sheffield Academic, 1996); Erhard S. Gerstenberger, *Psalms, Part 2, and Lamentations* (Grand Rapids: Eerdmans, 2001); and David Willgren [David Davage], *The Formation of the "Book" of Psalms: Reconsidering the Transmission and Canonization of Psalmody in Light of Material Culture and the Poetics of Anthologies* (Tübingen: Mohr Siebeck, 2016).
15. Willgren [Davage], *The Formation of the "Book" of Psalms*, 392.

Similarly, consider Psalms 23; 24; and 25. These three psalms can be read in conversation with one another, in sequence, building one off of another. When read together, they exhibit shared questions and answers, a deepening or broadening of a theological portrait of who God is and how God is with God's people, and a clear sense of the path set before the person who reads these psalms and what that can mean for that reader.

Psalm 23—a trust psalm—is a prayer spoken to God. The psalmist fears no evil, "for you [the LORD] are with me" (v. 4 AT). God is seen as a shepherd, a protector and caregiver. Psalm 24—an entrance liturgy—then advances this protective imagery, calling God the "King of glory," "strong and mighty, . . . mighty in battle" (v. 8 AT), who is at the same time the God "of salvation" (v. 5). Psalm 25—a praise psalm—then exults the Lord as the "God of *my* salvation" and a God of "friendship" (vv. 5, 14 AT).

Psalm 23, the psalm of trust, ends with the psalmist promising, "I shall dwell in [or "return to"] the house of the LORD all my life" (v. 6 AT). Psalm 24, which follows, is an entrance liturgy for the temple—that is, "the house of the LORD." Following on the heels of the promise to return to the house of the Lord in Psalm 23, the next psalm gives words asking to enter into that house: "Who shall ascend the hill of the LORD? And who shall stand in his holy place?" (24:3). A part of the answer to this question is, "Those who . . . do not lift up their souls to that which is false" (24:4 AT). Psalm 25 then prays, "To you, O LORD, I lift up my soul. . . . Guide me in your truth" (vv. 1, 5a AT).

Read together as a sequence, these three psalms offer a more comprehensive theological picture than any one of them paints alone. The composite theology of these psalms forms a picture of a God who is shepherd, king, and friend—a God who provides. God's provision looks like still waters and right pathways (23:2–3), blessing and vindication (24:5), relief from troubles and a bringing out from distress (25:17). All of this is done in the context of the psalmists' trust that "surely goodness and steadfast love shall pursue me" (23:6 AT) and the plea to God, "Remember your mercy, O LORD, and your steadfast love" (25:6 AT). The *ḥesed* of this shepherd/king/friend drives the theological picture.

Another interrelated feature of these three psalms is the question of the "right path." At the beginning of Psalm 23, the psalmist praises God, the good shepherd, for leading him in right paths. Psalm 25 takes up this image in greater detail, with the psalmist asking to be taught those paths (25:4) and to be led in God's truth (25:5), because this is who God is and how God relates to those who seek God out:

[8] The Lord is good and upright,
   therefore he instructs sinners *in the way.*
[9] He leads the humble in what is right,
   and teaches the poor his way.
[10] All *the paths of the* Lord are steadfast love and faithfulness,
   for those who keep his covenant and his decrees. (25:8–10 AT)

In between these two psalms, as noted above, Psalm 24 asks a question that Psalm 23 assumes and Psalm 25 asks for. Psalm 24 asks,

[3] Who shall ascend the mountain of the Lord?
   And who shall stand in his holy place? (v. 3)

Who? The answer quickly follows:

[4] Those who have clean hands and pure hearts,
   who do not lift up their souls to what is false,
   and do not swear deceitfully. (v. 4)

Psalm 25 then begins with this claim, which can be fruitfully read as a response to the question and answer in Psalm 24:

[1] To you, O Lord, I lift up my soul. (25:1)

Who will ascend the hill of the Lord, and who will stand in God's holy place? Who will "dwell in [or "return to"] the house of the Lord"? (Both psalms are clearly speaking here of the temple.) Those who "do not lift up their souls to what is false," comes the answer. And so the psalmist says, "I lift up my soul to you, O Lord." Psalm 23 assumes that God is present and that one will abide in God's house forever. Psalm 24 asks the question of who is worthy to be in God's presence, to enter God's temple. Psalm 25 states the intention that the psalmist desires to be made worthy to be in God's presence, adding a summary of sorts, an echoing question and answer to that of 24:4:

Who is the one who fears the Lord?
   He will teach that one the way a person should choose. (25:12 AT)

The careful, close reader will likely find other connections between these three psalms, but these are offered as examples of how reading these psalms together, as a sequence, can offer surprising moments of integration and new meanings.

## THE CHIASTIC STRUCTURE
## OF PSALMS 15–24

A growing number of scholars accept Psalms 3–14 and 15–24 as intentionally arranged groups within Book I of the Psalter. The French scholar Pierre Auffret was the first to argue that Psalms 15–24 are arranged chiastically about Psalm 19, with the "form" of the psalm as the organizing category. Auffret's argument was greeted with caution at first but has largely been accepted by scholars such as Susan Gillingham and William Brown.[a] The structure of this group of psalms is understood as follows:

15  Entrance liturgy
16  Psalm of trust
17  Lament / prayer for deliverance
18  Royal psalm
19  Torah psalm
20–21  Royal psalms
22  Lament / prayer for deliverance
23  Psalm of trust
24  Entrance liturgy

An exacting reader might note that the chiasm doesn't quite work, since two psalms (Pss. 20–21) are needed to balance Psalm 18. But the argument is that Psalm 18 is both petition and answer; Psalms 20–21 together form a corresponding petition and answer. Brown visually imagines this sequence on its side and sees Psalm 19 as the "top." He concludes,

> In the entrance liturgies [Pss. 14 and 25], moral qualifications are stipulated for admission into God's sanctuary. Psalm 23 concludes with the speaker's goal to dwell forever in the "house of YHWH." . . . Psalm 19 establishes both the goal of the reader's ascent within the collection and the entry point of the community into life before God. As the community bears witness to the King of glory at his entrance into the temple (24:8–10), so all of creation bears witness to the God of glory at the breaking of the dawn. All in all, Psalm 19 provides the highest possible yet most personal vantage point for witnessing, indeed bearing, God's effulgent presence.[b]

a. Pierre Auffret, *La sagesse a bâti sa maison: Études de structures littéraires dans l'Ancien Testament et spécialment dan les Psaumes* (Fribourg: Editions Universitaires, 1982); Susan Gillingham, *Psalms through the Centuries* (Oxford: Blackwell, 2008; Hoboken, NJ: Wiley Blackwell, 2018–22), 2:101–64; and William P. Brown, *Psalms*, Interpreting Biblical Texts (Nashville: Abingdon, 2010), 97–100.
b. Brown, *Psalms*, 106–7.

## GOING DEEPER

To deepen your grasp of the concepts introduced in this chapter, consider doing one or more of the following exercises:

1. Read Psalms 1 and 150. Think of Psalm 1 as the introduction to the book of Psalms. Write three sentences about what the image of the tree and the image of the "way [road] of the righteous" might mean as an invitation to read the psalms. Think of Psalm 150 as the final "exclamation point" on the end of the Psalter. Write two sentences about what the multiple "calls to praise" in Psalm 150 mean as a conclusion of the Psalter.

2. Consider either one of your favorite musical albums or playlists. Listen to the first three songs and think of them as an intentional sequence (rather than just as three random songs). How do the three songs build on one another? How does the third song sound different as a response to the first two? How would it sound if it were the first song rather than the third?

3. What are your three favorites jokes? Tell  those three jokes to a friend. In what order did you tell the jokes? And why? Ask your friend what order they would tell those jokes in. What difference does the order of the jokes make to their combined meaning?

## FOR FURTHER READING

deClaissé-Walford, Nancy, ed. *The Shape and Shaping of the Book of Psalms: The Current State of Scholarship.* Macon, GA: SBL Press, 2014.

Gillingham, Susan. *Psalms through the Centuries.* 3 vols. Oxford: Blackwell, 2008; Hoboken, NJ: Wiley Blackwell, 2018–22.

Howard, David M., Jr., and Andrew J. Schmutzer, eds. *Reading the Psalms Theologically.* Bellingham, WA: Lexham Academic, 2023.

Willgren, David [David Davage]. *The Formation of the "Book" of Psalms: Reconsidering the Transmission and Canonization of Psalmody in Light of Material Culture and the Poetics of Anthologies.* Tübingen: Mohr Siebeck, 2016.

Wilson, Gerald H. *The Editing of the Hebrew Psalter.* Chico, CA: Scholars Press, 1985.

## SEVEN

# "Who Is the King of Glory?"

*Learning to Understand the Theology of the Psalms*

The psalms are about life. But even more so, the psalms are about the life of faith. They are about life in relationship with God, about life in the midst of God's good-but-fallen creation, about life in community with God's good-but-sinful people. As William Brown has written, "Common to all the various genres and collections that constitute the Psalter is their primary object of discourse, God, who is as irreducibly complex as the psalms are literarily diverse."[1] All of which is to say that *the psalms are about God*. The prayers for help are prayed in the belief that such pleas are heard by the Lord, who is capable of answering those prayers. The psalms of praise are testimony about the actions and character of the Lord, whose hand has intruded into history and whose heart is steering history toward a purposeful goal. The psalms of instruction are lessons learned about the walk of faith in relationship with Israel's God. The psalms of trust express confidence in the presence of God amid circumstances that often seem to indicate the absence of God. And so on.

All of this leads to a basic question. Psalm 24:10 asks the question this way: "Who is this King of glory?" (AT). Who is the God of the psalms?

1. William P. Brown, *Seeing the Psalms: A Theology of Metaphor* (Louisville: Westminster John Knox, 2002), 137.

161

Psalm 24 also answers its own question: "The Lᴏʀᴅ of hosts, he is the King of glory" (v. 10). But can we say more? Who is the God to whom Israel prayed, in whom Israel trusted, about whom Israel testified, and under whose guidance Israel walked the walk of faith? Who is the God of the Psalter?

When we start to deal with this question, we are moving into the realm of *theology*. One classical definition of theology (from Anselm [died 1109]) is "faith seeking understanding" (*fides quaerens intellectum*).[2] Theology is the discipline of studying the whole "God question": God's person, God's ways of acting, and our relationship with God. When we talk about the "theology of the psalms," we are focusing more specifically on what the psalms have to say about the God question.

Or, as Psalm 24 puts it, "Who is the King of glory?"

To tackle this question, we must direct our questions about God to the 150 poems of the Psalter. Because these poems were not all written by the same person, there will be diversity. To use a metaphor, the picture of God that emerges from a study of the Psalter will be more like a mosaic than an oil painting. In an oil painting, the artist blends a palette of colors and controls the lines, the curves, and the shades. The picture that emerges is a unity. A viewer who takes in the picture may not notice the individual paints that were blended into the picture, precisely because they have been blended. In a mosaic, the artist uses preexisting chunks of stone, glass, or pottery and quite literally pieces them together to create an image. In this sort of picture, the lines tend to be a little more choppy: a viewer can still discern the shapes, colors, and lines of each individual piece of stone, glass, or pottery.

In the theology of the psalms, the task of the interpreter is to piece together a picture of God from the preexisting poems. And just as no two artists would create exactly the same image out of a set of 150 bits of colored glass, so also no two readers of the book of Psalms create exactly the same portrait of God out of the 150 psalms of the Psalter. What is offered here is our attempt to assemble a portrait of God from the 150 poems of the Psalter. Our portrait is not offered as the one-and-only theology of the psalms but as an invitation to you the reader to join the artistry, an invitation to join us in reading the psalms and creating your own portrait of the God whom we meet there. This chapter is an invitation to join in the conversation of *faith seeking understanding*.

---

2. See Daniel Migliore, *Faith Seeking Understanding: An Introduction to Christian Theology*, 2nd ed. (Grand Rapids: Eerdmans, 2004), 2.

# DEADWOOD AND PSALM 24

In season 1, episode 3, of the HBO series *Deadwood*, there is a split scene in which Reverend H. W. Smith (played by Ray McKinnon) presides over the burial of a criminal who has been killed, and then reflects on God's direction for people with the camp's not-yet but soon-to-be sheriff, Seth Bullock (played by Timothy Oliphant). At the burial, Reverend Smith recites a pieced-together version of Psalm 24 (vv. 1–5, 7, 10), and adds to it a similar patchwork reference to Proverbs 16 (vv. 5–7):

> ¹The earth is the LORD's and all that is in it,
>> the world, and those who live in it;
> ² for he has founded it on the seas,
>> and established it on the rivers.
>
> ³ Who shall ascend the hill of the LORD?
>> And who shall stand in his holy place?
> ⁴ Those who have clean hands and pure hearts,
>> who do not lift up their souls to what is false,
>> and do not swear deceitfully.
> ⁵ They will receive blessing from the LORD,
>> and vindication from the God of their salvation. . . .
>
> ⁷ Lift up your heads, O gates!
>> and be lifted up, O ancient doors!
>> that the King of glory may come in. . . .
> ¹⁰ Who is this King of glory?
>> The LORD of hosts,
>> he is the King of glory.
>
> ⁵ All those who are arrogant are an abomination to the LORD;
>> be assured, they will not go unpunished.
> ⁶ By loyalty and faithfulness iniquity is atoned for,
>> and by the fear of the LORD one avoids evil.
> ⁷ When the ways of people please the LORD,
>> he causes even their enemies to be at peace with them.

After the burial, Smith and Bullock are walking together, and Smith, sensing Bullock's unease with his role in the criminal's death, reflects on his own calling, and the calling of Bullock as well, apparently ruminating on the psalm's question, "Who shall ascend the hill of the LORD?" and its answer, "Those who have clean hands and pure hearts."

Smith: I was a field nurse during the war, at Shiloh and Second Manassas. That was a good deal of violence.

Bullock: Is that when you got your calling?

Smith: Yes it was, sir. Out of that crucible, out of all that horror to come to God's grace. . . . "A man's heart deviseth his way: but the Lord directeth his steps" [Prov. 16:9]. He directeth all our steps, Mr. Bullock. All of us.

Bullock: If you're preaching at me, Rev., you need to put some more light on the text.

Smith: If I am preaching at you, sir, I do you a disservice.

## The Assumption behind the Poems: The Faithfulness of God

One way to approach the question of the theology of the psalms is to come at the question in this way: Is there one fundamental assumption about God that all of the 150 poems of the Psalter share? Or to put it another way, if we carefully study all of the poems, prayers, and praise songs of the Psalter, is there any assertion about God that could serve as "background" to the entire collection?

The following verses have been drawn from different types of psalms: prayers for help, hymns of praise, songs of thanksgiving, psalms of trust, instructional psalms, and so on. Scan these verses and note any common elements that appear in all of the verses:

> For great is his loving faithfulness (*ḥesed*) toward us,
> and the truthfulness (*'emet*) of the LORD endures forever. (117:2 AT)

> Lord, where is your loving faithfulness of old,
> which you swore to David by your truthfulness? (89:49 AT)

> Let your face shine upon your servant;
> in your loving faithfulness, save me! (31:16 AT)

> I am like a thriving olive tree in the house of God;
> I trust in the loving faithfulness of God forever. (52:8 AT)

> [God] has magnified the deliverance of his king;
> he has shown loving faithfulness to his anointed one. (18:50 AT)

> Truly God has listened;
> God has attended to the sound of my prayer!
> Praised be God, who has not rejected my prayer,
> or taken his loving faithfulness from me! (66:19–20 AT)

> Many are the woes of the wicked person,
> But the one who trusts in the LORD is surrounded by loving
> faithfulness. (32:10 AT)

> Let them thank the LORD for his loving faithfulness,
> for his wonderful works to humanity. (107:8, 15, 21, 31 AT)

Quite obviously, these verses were carefully selected to show a pattern. For that reason, the reader ought to proceed with a good bit of skepticism about what is coming next. That is, the data above have been rather drastically skewed to lead to the conclusion that we want readers to draw. So let us lay our cards on the table about what conclusion we hope readers will draw. Each of these verses contains a term that we believe is the fundamental theological assumption that hovers behind all of the psalms. And that assumption is this: *The Lord is a God of loving faithfulness.*[3] Even though the verses were cherry-picked to support the conclusion we want readers to reach, the rest of the chapter will show (we hope) that there is a great deal more support for this conclusion than just the above verses. We believe that the Psalter as a whole assumes the basic conviction that Israel believed in "a God of loving faithfulness."

So, let us dig a little more deeply into this word *ḥesed*. The phrase "loving faithfulness" actually translates a single Hebrew word: *ḥesed*.

In the Old Testament, the word describes both God's *internal character* as well as the *fundamental characteristics of God's external actions*. Both God's character and God's characteristic actions are defined by this word: *ḥesed*.

No single English word is an equivalent for this Hebrew word. For that reason, translators generally rely on a range of words and use whatever word seems to fit best in a given context. The stock of words that have been used to translate the Hebrew word *ḥesed* into English include these: "love," "faithfulness/fidelity," "kindness," "loyalty," "commitment," and "mercy." Oftentimes scholars combine words in the attempt to nuance the translation: "loving-kindness," "steadfast love," "sovereign love," "covenant love," and (as we have opted for here) "loving faithfulness." Katharine Doob Sakenfeld, who has studied the word more deeply than any other scholar, has recently written that *ḥesed*

> is generally used in the OT in the context of a relationship where one person is in significant need of help from the other, help that typically may be beyond the usual expectations of such a relationship, and help that often is essential to the basic well-being or even the survival of the needy person. The word may also be used to express *the ongoing attitude and continuing acts done by one person for another in support and maintenance of their relationship*. . . . When used of God, [*ḥesed*] lifts up *the foundational commitment God has made in covenant to the Israelite community*.[4]

This word is one of the most important and most theologically laden terms in the Old Testament. The importance of this term, along with a small

3. For a more technical version of this argument, see Rolf A. Jacobson, "'The Faithfulness of the Lord Endures Forever': The Theological Witness of the Psalter," in *Soundings in the Theology of the Psalms: Perspectives and Methods in Contemporary Scholarship*, ed. Rolf A. Jacobson (Minneapolis: Fortress, 2011), 111–38.

4. Katharine Doob Sakenfeld, "Khesed," in *The New Interpreter's Dictionary of the Bible* (Nashville: Abingdon, 2008), 3:495–96 (emphasis added). See also Sakenfeld, *The Meaning of Hesed in the Hebrew Bible: A New Inquiry* (Missoula, MT: Scholars Press, 1978).

constellation of related terms, can be gleaned by an examination of Exodus 34:6–7. Walter Brueggemann has described this passage as "one of the most remarkable and important utterances in the OT."[5] The passage consists of one of the most ancient, creedlike fragments in the Bible—a creedal artifact, as it were, from the earliest days of Israel's relationship with the Lord. In the passage, the Lord speaks these words about the Lord's own self. In other words, "the speech in verses 6–7 is Yahweh's self-disclosure, revealing to Moses the fullness of God's character and intentionality."[6]

> The LORD passed before [Moses], and proclaimed,
>> "The LORD, the LORD, a God merciful and gracious,
>> slow to anger,
>> and abounding in loving faithfulness [ḥesed] and truthfulness,
>> keeping loving faithfulness [ḥesed] to the thousandth generation,
>> forgiving iniquity and transgression and sin,
>> yet by no means clearing the guilty,
>> but visiting the iniquity of the parents
>> upon the children
>> and the children's children,
>> to the third and fourth generation." (vv. 6–7 AT)

In the context of Exodus 34, the forgiving character of the Lord is especially prominent—the Lord remembers sin "to the third and fourth generation" but forgives and is faithful "to the thousandth generation." The context of the story also emphasizes the Lord's compassionate forgiveness. No sooner had God entered into a covenant relationship with Israel (Exod. 19–20, 24) than Israel sinned and broke the covenant by worshiping a graven image (Exod. 32). Moses pleads with the Lord for mercy. The Lord answers Moses's intercession, reissues the Ten Commandments, renews the covenant, and issues the above "self-disclosure."

Israel forever afterward carried this creedlike fragment and treasured it as its dominant confession about who the Lord is. Variations of this foundational confession may be found throughout the Old Testament (Num. 14:18; Neh. 9:17; Jer. 32:18; Joel 2:13; Jon. 4:2), and also, most significantly for our purposes, in the Psalter: 86:15; 103:8; and 145:8. The central verse of the confession, that the Lord is a God of "loving faithfulness [ḥesed] and truthfulness [ʾemet]," became an abbreviated shorthand for Israel. This is apparent

---

5. Walter Brueggemann, "Exodus: Introduction, Commentary, and Reflections," in *The New Interpreter's Bible: A Commentary in 12 Volumes* (Nashville: Abingdon, 1994), 1:946.
6. Brueggemann, "Exodus," 946.

especially in the Psalter, where the two terms appear together seventeen times, as they do in the shortest of all psalms, Psalm 117:

> For great is his loving faithfulness [*ḥesed*] toward us,
>> and the truthfulness [*'emet*] of the LORD endures forever. (v. 2 AT)[7]

The single term "loving faithfulness" (*ḥesed*), moreover, becomes an even briefer shorthand summary of Israel's faith: "His loving faithfulness [*ḥesed*] endures forever" (Ps. 118:1). This exact phrase alone occurs thirty-two times in the Psalter. The Psalter, more than any other book of the Bible, uses this term to describe God's character and God's characteristic ways of acting and being in relationship with God's people.

By means of this term, then, Israel bore witness to the Lord as a God who is in relationships for the long haul. Once the Lord enters into a relationship, the Lord is in it for good. Nothing can make God give up on the relationship. And the Lord is willing to do whatever it takes to maintain, refresh, or renew the relationship: this includes forgiving sins, loving unconditionally, and offering second and third and fourth chances.

## The Faithfulness of God and the Genres of the Psalms

Above, there was a list of verses gathered together from all of the basic genres of the psalms—from prayers for help, songs of thanksgiving, hymns of praise, psalms of trust, instructional psalms, and so on. And in each verse the basic term *ḥesed* (loving faithfulness) occurs. A next question to wonder about might be this: How does the basic assumption that Israel's God was a God of loving faithfulness work in each of the different genres?

If we scan each of the major genres of the psalms, we can see how each genre, in its own way, works a bit differently with Israel's basic theological confession that the Lord is a God of faithfulness. In the next section we will explore how this basic theological confession is worked a bit differently in the main genres of the Psalter.

### The Lord's Loving Faithfulness and the Hymns of Praise

As the reader will recall, the normal pattern of the hymns of praise is twofold: an initial *call to praise* is followed by *reasons for praise* (these reasons are normally introduced by the Hebrew word *ki*, translated below as "for").

---

7. This word pairing also occurs in Pss. 25:5–6, 10; 26:3; 31:1–8; 40:10–11; 57:10; 61:7; 69:13; 85:11; 86:15; 89:14; 108:4; 115:1; 117:2; 138:2.

With that form as background, consider the opening verses of Psalms 106; 107; 117; 118; and 136:

> Praise the LORD!
> Give testimony to the LORD, for he is good;
>> *for his loving faithfulness endures forever!* (106:1 AT)
>
> Give testimony to the LORD, for he is good;
>> *for his loving faithfulness endures forever!* (107:1 AT)
>
> Praise the LORD, all you nations!
>> Extol him, all you peoples!
> *For his loving faithfulness is great onto us,*
>> and his truthfulness endures forever.
> Praise the LORD! (117:1–2 AT)
>
> Give testimony to the LORD, for he is good,
>> *For his loving faithfulness endures forever!*
>
> Let Israel say,
>> *"His loving faithfulness endures forever!"*
> Let the house of Aaron say,
>> *"His loving faithfulness endures forever!"*
> Let those who fear the LORD say,
>> *"His loving faithfulness endures forever!"* (118:1–4 AT)
>
> Give testimony to the LORD, for he is good,
>> *for his loving faithfulness endures forever!*
> Give testimony to the God of gods,
>> *for his loving faithfulness endures forever!*
> Give testimony to the Lord of lords
>> *for his loving faithfulness endures forever!* (136:1–3 AT [the phrase
>> repeats in every verse of the psalm])

What these verses demonstrate is that when Israel needed a singular reason for praise that sums up all of the other reasons for praise, the following phrase did the job: "*the loving faithfulness of the* LORD *endures forever.*"

A close examination of all of the hymns of praise, furthermore, identifies two broad domains in which the Lord's loving faithfulness is proven, two areas in which the loving commitment of the Lord can be experienced: in creation and in history.

The first domain in which the psalms testify to having experienced God's loving faithfulness is creation. In the words of Psalm 136, the Lord is the one who has fashioned a trustworthy creation out of chaos,

> who made the heavens through understanding,
> > for his loving faithfulness endures forever;
> who spread out the earth on the waters,
> > for his loving faithfulness endures forever;
> who made the great lights,
> > for his loving faithfulness endures forever. (vv. 5–7 AT)

As the repetition of the phrase "for his loving faithfulness endures forever" indicates, the very existence of a safe and trustworthy creation in which life can flourish is a testimony to the creator's faithfulness. As creator of all, the Lord has fashioned an orderly and thus trustworthy creation. The Lord has "set a boundary that [the forces of chaos] may not pass" (Ps. 104:9a).[8] Within this realm, order exists. This order in turn encompasses time, which has both daily and seasonal rhythms: "You have made the moon to mark the seasons; the sun knows its time for setting" (v. 19). The daily rhythm allows for human and animal life to live mutually: "When the sun rises, [the wild animals] withdraw. . . . People go out to do their work and to labor until the evening" (vv. 22a–23). The seasonal rhythm allows for the harvests that sustain God's creatures: "You cause the grass to grow for the cattle, and plants for people to use, to bring forth food from the earth" (vv. 14–15a). God's order also includes spatial dimensions: places for sun, moon, air, and water but also places for wild animals (trees in which "birds build their nests," "high mountains . . . for the wild goats," and so on; vv. 17–18).

The second domain in which God's loving faithfulness can be experienced, according to the psalms, is history—specifically in the history of God's relationship with the nation of Israel. Within history, the psalms testify, God has proved to be faithful by being faithful to Abraham and Sarah's descendants.

> It is he who remembered us in our low estate,
> > for his loving faithfulness endures forever;
> and rescued us from our foes,
> > for his loving faithfulness endures forever. (136:23–24 AT)

Two aspects of Israel's history with God are highlighted in the Psalter. First, the psalms testify that Israel's history with God was purely a matter of divine grace and forgiveness. Israel's history tells the long and sad story about

---

8. In the psalms, as in the rest of the Old Testament and indeed throughout the ancient Near East, waters and the sea are understood as the embodiment of chaos, as the physical form of the disorderly powers that resist God's ordering creative powers.

how Israel consistently proved unfaithful to God: "They did not remember the greatness of your loving faithfulness" (106:7 AT). "They were rebellious in their intentions" (v. 43 AT). Yet the Lord was forgiving because it is God's nature to keep promises and to show loving faithfulness in forgiveness: "For their sake he remembered his covenant, and showed compassion according to the greatness of his loving faithfulness" (v. 45 AT).

Second, in Israel's history God's loving faithfulness often took the form of wondrous acts—acts of power that are beyond human ability or comprehension. These actions include first and foremost the promises that God made to Abraham and Sarah: "the covenant that he made with Abraham, his sworn promise to Isaac" (Ps. 105:9). In theological terms, this action is referred to as "election": God's act of choosing Abraham and Sarah and their descendants (see vv. 12–15). And because God first chose Abraham and Sarah and then remained faithful to their descendants, God proved faithful to them in many other wondrous acts of deliverance and rescue: the Lord "remembered his holy promise, and Abraham his servant" (v. 42). These actions include rescuing the people from slavery in Egypt, the gift of the covenant, the gift of the law, guidance through the wilderness, the gift of the promised land, the choice of David as the founder of the enduring monarchy, and the choice of Jerusalem as the place where God's "name" would dwell.[9]

### The Lord's Loving Faithfulness and the Prayers for Help

If the hymns of praise offer testimony about God's character and the character of God's actions in history and creation, the prayers for help can be described as offering what the prominent Old Testament scholar Walter Brueggemann called "countertestimony."[10] In this countertestimony, Israel "cross-examines" its own testimony about the Lord "in order to inquire into its adequacy, coherence, credibility, and congruence." According to Brueggemann, the "high claims of the core testimony" of Israel require the freedom to question those claims. In order to be trustworthy, a person's testimony must be allowed to be questioned. Any authority that refuses to allow its construal of reality to be questioned is untrustworthy. In this regard, it is significant to observe that in the prayers for help, the Lord *invites* hard questions and even denunciations from the people.

In the prayers for help, those ancient sufferers at the same time paradoxically both *question God's loving faithfulness* and *make God's loving*

---

9. See here the texts of the historical psalms: Pss. 78; 89; 105; 106; 107; 132.

10. See Walter Brueggemann, *Old Testament Theology: Testimony, Dispute, Advocacy* (Minneapolis: Fortress, 1996), 317 (and all of chap. 8).

*faithfulness the basis of their hope and their prayers.* Psalm 89:49 may be the most strident complaint verse in the Psalter. This verse is the turning point of Psalm 89, the last psalm in Book III of the Psalter—a psalm that some scholars see as the turning point of the entire Psalter.[11] In this verse, the sufferer questions God's commitment and fidelity to the people: "LORD, where is your loving faithfulness of old, which you swore to David by your truthfulness?" (AT). Or again, this time in a communal prayer for help, "Has God's loving faithfulness ceased forever? Are God's promises ended for all time?" (77:8 AT). Other questioning verses maintain the same sort of accusation against God:

> My God, my God, why have you forsaken me? (22:1)

> Why, O LORD, do you stand far off? (10:1)

> Why do you sleep, O LORD? (44:23)

> Will you forget me forever? (13:1)

> How long, O LORD, will you look on [but do nothing]? (35:17)

In the context of these strong questions put to God, questions that border on accusations, it is even more striking that the prayers for help nonetheless maintain that their only hope is God's loving faithfulness. Notice how in all of the following request-for-help verses of lament psalms, no matter what unique crisis the psalmist is in, the Lord's loving faithfulness is the basis for the psalmist's request. What follows are just a few of the many examples of petitions from the Psalter's prayers for help.

In Psalm 17, a sufferer seeking rescue from oppressing enemies prays,

> Wondrously show your loving faithfulness,
> O savior of those who seek refuge from their adversaries. (v. 7 AT)

In Psalm 31, a person who was likely suffering from a debilitating disease prays,

> Let your face shine upon your servant,
> In your loving faithfulness, save me! (v. 16 AT)

---

11. See Gerald H. Wilson, *The Editing of the Hebrew Psalter* (Chico, CA: Scholars Press, 1985), 212–28; and Wilson, "The Use of Royal Psalms at the Seams of the Hebrew Psalter," *Journal for the Study of the Old Testament* 35 (1986): 85–94.

In Psalm 40, a sufferer who is beset by both sins and oppressors prays,

> Do not, O LORD, withhold your mercy from me;
> > let your loving faithfulness and your truth keep me safe forever.
> > > (v. 11 AT)

In Psalm 44, a communal psalm, the entire community prays for deliverance from a national enemy:

> Rise up, come to our aid.
> > Rescue us for the sake of your loving faithfulness. (v. 26 AT)

In Psalm 69, a psalmist who is figuratively drowning in "waters that have come up to my neck" is claiming innocence with regard to sins and prays,

> But I, my prayer is to you, O LORD!
> > At the right moment, answer me, O God,
> > in the greatness of your loving faithfulness. (v. 13 AT)

In Psalm 109, a person who has been falsely accused of a crime prays,

> Help me, O LORD my God!
> > Save me according to your loving faithfulness. (v. 26 AT)

And in Psalms 25 and 51, two psalmists who are guilty of sin pray for forgiveness:

> Be mindful of your mercy, O LORD,
> > and of your loving faithfulness, for they are from of old.
> Do not remember the sins of my youth or my transgressions;
> > according to your loving faithfulness remember me,
> > for the sake of your goodness, O LORD! (25:6–7 AT)

> Have mercy on me, O God,
> > according to your loving faithfulness;
> according to your abundant mercy
> > blot out my sins. (51:1 AT)

What ties all of the above pleas together is the common theological basis on which they make their requests: *the loving faithfulness of the Lord*. The above psalms are prayed from a variety of crisis situations. The requests that they make of God take a variety of forms. The voices that spoke these psalms were different. But the grounds on which the psalmists dare to hope are the same. If we zero in on just the last two examples cited above, we notice that the request for forgiveness is based solely on the Lord's loving faithfulness. Rather than basing the request for forgiveness on the psalmist's actions—such as a promise not to sin again, or a vow to engage in conciliatory good works to atone for the past sin, or going through a set of rituals meant to show repentance, or an extended time of self-punishment to show true contrition—the psalmist places the burden on the Lord's character as a merciful, gracious, faithful God.

The prayers for help thus present a paradox. On the one hand, in the complaint elements of these prayers, God's loving faithfulness is questioned. Those who suffer do challenge God, testifying that the suffering they are experiencing is at odds with Israel's testimony to the faithfulness of the Lord. On the other hand, in the petition elements of these prayers, the psalmists completely rely on the Lord's loving faithfulness. Whether the psalmists are praying for forgiveness, begging to be healed, seeking vindication from a false accusation, or asking for deliverance from oppressors, they consistently base their requests on the faithful character of the Lord. It is in this ambiguous reality—paradoxically both questioning and relying on the Lord's fidelity—that the prayers for help do their theology. They teach us that *doubt is a part of living* with faith and that *living with questions is part of the answer* that biblical religion provides.

### The Lord's Loving Faithfulness and the Psalms of Trust

While the hymns of praise offer testimony about God's character, and the prayers for help simultaneously question the Lord's faithfulness and yet rely on that faithfulness, the psalms of trust completely give themselves over to God's loving fidelity. Chapter 2 introduced the reader to trust psalms. Like the prayers for help, the trust psalms are prayed in the midst of a situation of crisis. But whereas the prayers for help express faith by dwelling deeply in the questions, the trust psalms (as the name indicates) are marked by their mood of trust. With metaphorical flourish, the trust psalms name the clear and present dangers that surround life, such as "the valley of the shadow of death" (23:4 KJV), "evildoers [who] assail me to devour my flesh" (27:2), "the mountains [that] shake in the heart of the sea" (46:2). But with equal metaphorical flourish, the trust psalms assert confidence in the Lord, who is described as "my shepherd" (23:1), "my light and my salvation" (27:1), "our refuge and strength" (46:1), and so on.

As one might expect, the reason the trust psalms give for being able to trust in the midst of crisis is the faithful character of the Lord. In the following examples, taken from trust psalms or from trust sections of other psalms, observe how these poems bear witness to God's character, but also notice the elegant metaphorical descriptions of God's presence and power:

> Why do you boast of your evil, brave fellow?
> God's faithfulness never ceases! . . .
> But I am like a thriving olive tree in God's house;
> I trust in the faithfulness of God forever and ever. (52:1, 8 NJPS)

> [God] sends from heaven and saves me,
> rebuking those who hotly pursue me—
> God sends forth his love and faithfulness. . . .
> For great is your love, reaching to the heavens;
> your faithfulness reaches to the skies. (57:3, 10 NIV)

> My God in his loving faithfulness will meet me;
> God will let me look down on those who slander me. (59:10 AT)

> One thing God has promised, and two things I have heard,
> that power belongs to God,
> and loving faithfulness belongs to you, O Lord. (62:11–12a AT)

> Because your loving faithfulness is better than life itself,
> my lips praise you! (63:3 AT)

> Loving faithfulness and truthfulness have met each other;
> righteousness and peace have kissed!
> Truthfulness springs up from the ground,
> and righteousness looks down from the heavens! (85:10–11 AT)

Examples could be multiplied, but these are enough to drive home the point. In the psalms of trust, the poets do not merely express trust; they also bear proud witness to the reason they are able to trust: the loving, faithful character of the Lord. "Trust" is not brave courage in the face of adversity—at least, not if we understand courage to be some quality of personality that a person stirs up from within. It would be a significant misreading of these psalms to interpret them as saying that the psalmists mustered up their own courage, or as telling us that we need to have faith amid trials. Rather, the psalms understand trust as a response to a promise from God. These poets imagine courage in the midst of chaos not as the result of intestinal fortitude but as an unexpected miracle, sparked by the faithful activity of God. If left to rely on their own resources, the psalmists know that "they are like a dream, like grass that is renewed in the morning, but which by the evening has faded and withered" (90:5 AT). But "under his wings" and behind God's "shield and buckler" (91:4), the psalmists know that they need "not fear the terror of the night, or the arrow that flies by day, or the pestilence that stalks in the darkness, or the destruction that lays waste at [high noon]" (vv. 5–6).

As explored in chapter 5, one of the primary ways in which the psalms as a whole make meaning is through metaphor. This is true of the theological meaning of the psalms, and it is especially true of the trust psalms. The deep metaphors and rich imagery of the psalms do not serve simply as the icing on the Psalter's cake: instead, the metaphors and imagery are the thing itself. As William Brown has stated, "One must be careful, however, to guard against the still prevalent notion that images serve only to 'dress up ideas.'"[12] The images or metaphors that the psalmists employ to express their trust in God is part and parcel of the meaning: one cannot be separated from the other. The image, such as the shepherd who guides the sheep to green pastures, conveys not just an idea to an audience, but an *experience*. This experience is part of the theological witness of the psalms, and especially of the trust psalms. The trust psalms evoke emotions of terror and insecurity as they name the threatening realities of life in the real world. But the trust psalms also evoke trust and confidence as they depict the Lord metaphorically as light, shepherd, fortress, protecting wing, shadow, shield, and so on. To read these psalms is to experience the comfort that these images offer and to take hold of the promises of protection and guidance that such images imply.

### The Lord's Loving Faithfulness and the Songs of Thanksgiving

A final psalm form considered here in relation to the dominant theological confession of the Psalter is the song of thanksgiving. When the song of thanksgiving was introduced in chapter 2, the similarity that this form bears to the hymn of praise was mentioned. Like the hymn of praise, the intent of the song of thanksgiving is to praise the Lord as a means of bearing witness to what the Lord has done. But whereas the hymn of praise addresses God's more general works, such as creation or events in the distant past of Israel's history with God, the song of thanksgiving bears witness to more concrete, current, and particular experiences of God's faithfulness, such as recovery from an illness or rescue from an oppressor's attack. The song of thanksgiving also bears a close relationship to the prayer for help. The prayer for help is prayed

---

12. Brown, *Seeing the Psalms*, 11. The quotation within the quotation of Brown is from Luis Alonso Schökel, *A Manual of Hebrew Poetics* (1988; repr., Rome: Editrice Pontificio Istituto Biblico, 2000), 100.

in the midst of a crisis, and often the psalmist makes a "promise to praise" God once the crisis has passed. The song of thanksgiving is sung after the crisis has passed and is the psalmist's fulfillment of the promise to praise.

It should come as no surprise that when the psalmists look back on their experience of being rescued from a severe crisis, they credit their "deliverance from evil" to the loving faithfulness of God. Just as the sufferers in the prayers for help voice their reliance on God's loving faithfulness to get them out of the tight spot they are in, the singers of the songs of thanksgiving look back on the close call they had and say, "God's faithfulness saw me through it."

The first half of Psalm 40 clearly demonstrates how the songs of trust bear witness to the Lord's character. In the first five verses of the psalm, the singer narrates the escape from crisis: "I waited anxiously for the LORD," who "drew me up from the desolate pit." In the next verses, the psalmist presents personal praise as testimony to what God has done and who God is:

> I have delivered good news of righteousness
>     in the great congregation;
> I have not restrained my lips;
>     you know this, O LORD!
> I have not hidden your righteousness in the midst of my heart:
>     I have reported your truthfulness and your salvation.
> I have not concealed your loving faithfulness
>     or your fidelity from the great congregation. (vv. 9–10 AT)

Not only does the psalmist interpret the deliverance from evil as an instance of having personally experienced the Lord's "loving faithfulness," but the singer also understands the personal testimony to that experience as a means of grace through which the Lord's loving faithfulness is made available to others in the congregation. By singing about their own experiences of God's saving help, the songs of thanksgiving in turn mediate God's faithfulness to others. Below are examples from other songs of thanksgiving, in which the singers describe their experiences of deliverance as instances of God's loving faithfulness.

In Psalm 18, the king reports how God delivered him from a crisis:

> [God] has magnified the deliverance of his king;
>     he has shown loving faithfulness to his anointed one,
>     to David and to his offspring forever. (v. 50 AT)

In Psalm 21, another royal song of trust, the king's representative reports how God has delivered the king:

> For the king has trusted in the LORD,
> > in the loving faithfulness of the Most High he shall not be shaken.
> > (v. 7 AT)

Psalm 32 is a song of thanksgiving from one who has experienced forgiveness:

> Many are the woes of the wicked person,
> > but the one who trusts in the Lord is surrounded by loving
> > faithfulness. (v. 10 AT)

In Psalm 66, a song of thanksgiving, the singer celebrates God's deliverance of the people from a crisis and God's forgiveness:

> Truly God has listened;
> > God has attended to the sound of my prayer!

> Praised be God, who has not rejected my prayer,
> > or taken his loving faithfulness from me! (vv. 19–20 AT)

Psalm 92 is a song of thanksgiving sung by someone who has passed through an unnamed crisis and has come to the sanctuary with a purpose:

> to declare your loving faithfulness in the morning,
> > and your truthfulness by night. (v. 2 AT)

Psalm 107 is perhaps the most magnificent song of thanksgiving. In four parallel stanzas this communal song describes the loving faithfulness that Israel has experienced at the Lord's hands. The psalm begins with the familiar opening, "Give testimony to the LORD, for he is good; for his loving faithfulness endures forever!" (v. 1). Then, at the end of each of the four parallel stanzas, the psalmist sings:

> Let them thank the LORD for his loving faithfulness,
> > for his wonderful works to humanity. (vv. 8, 15, 21, 31 AT)

The psalm closes with a light variation on this theme:

> Let those who are wise keep these things,
> > and continually discern the loving faithfulness of the LORD. (v. 43 AT)

According to the songs of thanksgiving, the faithfulness of the Lord is an ever-flowing fountain, available to all who turn to God: "He turns a desert into pools of water, a parched land into springs of water" (107:35). The fountain flows not only for unfortunate human beings who are caught out in the desert but also for hungry people who live in hope of the harvest. The fountain flows for those who are imprisoned, exiled, or sick. It flows for the lowly, for sinners, and even for the upright of heart.

## God and the Faithfulness of God

The question of the theology of the psalms finally arrives at assertions about what kind of God the psalms presume. The exploration of this question is worthy of a lifetime of study, prayer, and conversation. The reader is invited into that lifetime conversation. Here we offer some summary reflections.

### A God Committed to All of Creation

The first reflection is that the psalms as a whole presume that the Lord is a God who is committed to all of creation. As one of us has written on a previous occasion, this might be described as "a larger web of fidelity." Individuals often wonder, "Why has God not been more faithful to me? Why hasn't God answered my prayer? If God is so faithful, why hasn't God given me what I want?" Yet we recognize that God is faithful not just to individuals but also to creation in all its complexity:

> God's faithfulness has formed a trustworthy creation, with laws and orders that offer a trustworthy environment in which life can teem. But to a believer who falls from a high precipice and cries out to God for deliverance (one thinks here of Ps. 91:12), God's fidelity to the law of gravity may not seem comforting. . . . The human creature tends to reduce God's fidelity to a single relational strand connecting God and the believer (or the believer's community). The Psalter, however, seems to paint God's fidelity as a web of relational commitments, in which the Lord remains faithful not only to one individual or one community but [also] to a dizzying array of creatures and creations.[13]

The faithfulness of God that the psalms proclaim is a faithfulness to the laws of creation as well as to the people whom God has chosen to bear God's name. This loving faithfulness may be witnessed not just in the history of Israel and of the church but also in the predictable laws and hierarchies of nature.

13. Jacobson, "'Faithfulness of the Lord Endures Forever,'" 155.

You have made the moon to mark the seasons,
    the sun knows its time for setting.
You make darkness, and it is night,
    when all the animals of the forest come creeping out.
The young lions roar for their prey,
    seeking their food from God.
When the sun rises,
    they withdraw and lie down in their dens.
People go out to their work
    and to their labor until the evening. (104:19–23)

### A God Who Does Not Mind Being Challenged

Any portrait of God that emerges from the psalms must deal with a central paradox of the Psalter. On the one hand, the poems of the Psalter maintain that the Lord is a God of loving faithfulness. On the other hand, both the individuals who belong to God and the community of people who belong to God often experience suffering. In the words of the prayers for help, God's people often experience circumstances that seem to contradict the tenet that the creator of life is a God of loving fidelity. The Psalter does not resolve the tension that exists between these two seemingly incompatible realities. Rather, it maintains that the life of faith is lived out in between these two sets of experiences: experiences of God as loving, as faithful, as true, as present with people, and experiences of suffering, of oppression, of evil.

What the Psalter does offer—in the prayers for help and the psalms of trust—are words for the faithful to take up and pray during such experiences, even to shout, to scream, to hurl at God. The theology of the Psalter maintains that the Lord does not mind it when God's people challenge God, or question God, or just plain yell at God in anger. God's loving faithfulness includes the invitation that when God's people talk to God, they can take off the gloves, as it were, and really let God have it. Where are you? Why did you let this happen? Where is your so-called loving faithfulness now? God can take such questions and challenges. God will not end God's relationship with a person or a people if they offer God questions rather than praise. In fact, God invites such challenges.

The book of Job, in fact, suggests that praying such challenging, questioning prayers is the proper way both for a person to suffer and for the rest of the community to accompany those who suffer. In the book that bears his name, Job is a righteous man who suffers greatly. Some of his friends—named Eliphaz, Bildad, and Zophar—come to be with Job in his suffering. But when Job curses the day of his birth and questions God, the friends grow uneasy and start to give Job advice about God. For most of the book, Job and his friends stay trapped in this cycle. Job questions and challenges God. The friends talk to Job and give advice. Near the end of the book, God speaks to Job. Yet at the very end, God also speaks to Eliphaz: "My anger burns against you and your two friends, because *you did not speak to me*, as is legitimate, as my servant Job did. Now . . . my servant Job shall pray for you, and I will accept his prayer not to deal with you according to your foolishness; *because you did not speak to me*, as is legitimate, as my servant Job did" (42:7–8 AT). Most versions err when rendering this passage and translating the words in italics as "you did not speak about me what is right." But these translations miss the fact that throughout the book, Job takes his complaints, questions, and challenges directly to God. Meanwhile, his friends, rather than praying with Job and on behalf of Job, give Job advice. They try to fix his theology. Job, as is legitimate, lives his theology—and complains to God.

Like the book of Job, the book of Psalms bears witness to a God who views challenges, questions, and even angry denunciations as legitimate. The God of the psalms invites us to live our theology in relationship with God—by praying not only words of trust and praise but also questions and challenges.

## WHERE IS GOD?

One theological concept that is important in the psalms is the "presence" and "absence" of God. Read the following select list of verses and ask, What do these verses say about God's presence? Where do they agree or disagree? How can the differences be explained?

> Why do the nations say,
>     "Where is their God?"
> Our God is in heaven,
>     he does whatever pleases him. (115:2–3 NIV)

> God is within [Jerusalem], she will not fall;
>     God will help her at the break of day. (46:5 NIV)

> Where can I go from your Spirit?
>     Where can I flee from your presence?
> If I go up to the heavens, you are there;
>     if I make my bed in the depths, you are there. (139:7–8 NIV)

> Send me your light and your faithful care,
>     let them lead me;
> let them bring me to your holy mountain,
>     to the place where you dwell. (43:3 NIV)

### A God Who Works through Others

The psalms also understand God's faithfulness as *a faithfulness that is often mediated through others*. That is, God often works through others. A creature might be the means by which God works faithfully at one moment, and yet that same creature might experience God's faithfulness through a different means at another moment.

The most prominent "agent" through whom God works in the Psalter is the human king. This is apparent especially in the royal psalms. The human king is accountable for the welfare of the entire people, for the entire land, and for all of the creatures that live in the land. Because of this, the psalms speak most often and most eloquently about the calling of the king as the means through which God's faithfulness is at work. This is apparent in the royal psalms as a whole, but especially so in Psalm 72, which is an intercessory prayer on behalf of the king as the agent of God's will:

> Give the king your justice, O God,
>     and your righteousness to a king's son.
> May he judge your people with righteousness,
>     and your poor with justice.
> May the mountains yield prosperity for the people,
>     and the hills, in righteousness.
> May he defend the cause of the poor of the people,
>     give deliverance to the needy,
>     and crush the oppressor. (vv. 1–4)

In the psalms, God also works through other agents, not all of them human. The city of Jerusalem, for example, is understood as a gift from God through which God continues to work:

> Walk about Zion, go all around it,
>     count its towers,
> consider well its ramparts;
>     go through its citadels,
> that you may tell the next generation
>     that this is God,
> our God forever and ever.
>     He will be our guide forever. (48:12–14)

The idea here is that the city is a means of God's grace and love—its walls, its streets, its roofs and houses. These things are not only of God but also of its government, its administration, its markets, and its laws. Such everyday, commonplace things are signs of God's faithfulness. What Martin Luther wrote in his Small Catechism about God the creator is a faithful summary of what the Psalter means about God's faithfulness as it comes to us through agents such as a ruler or a city: "God daily and abundantly provides shoes and clothing, food and drink, house and farm, spouse and children, fields, livestock, and all property—along with all the necessities and nourishment for this body and life."[14] As Luther's statement implies, God works not only through those with callings high in government or through the structures of national power but also through the callings of all people and through local structures: governmental structures, corporate structures, nonprofit organizations, and so on. God works through farmers and farms, through teachers and schools, through parents and homes. God's faithfulness flows through these agents when they are in turn faithful to God's law and are agents of God's love and justice.

### A God Active in the World

To maintain that God works through agents is not, however, to assert that God is not present in active and powerful ways. Often in the psalms, the "wicked" and the "enemies" assert that God is not an active agent in the world:

> In the pride of their countenance the wicked say, "God will not seek
>     it out";
>   all their thoughts are, "There is no God." (10:4)

> They think in their heart, "God has forgotten,
>   he has hidden his face, he will never see it." (10:11)

> Why do the wicked renounce God,
>   and say in their hearts, "You will not call us to account"? (10:13)

> There they are, bellowing with their mouths,
>   with sharp words on their lips—
>   for "Who," they think, "will hear us?" (59:7–8a)

> They hold fast to their evil purpose;
>   they talk of laying snares secretly,
> thinking, "Who can see us?" (64:5)

14. Martin Luther, "The Small Catechism," in *The Book of Concord: The Confessions of the Evangelical Lutheran Church*, ed. Robert Kolb and Timothy Wengert (Minneapolis: Fortress, 2000), 354.

> They say, "The LORD does not see;
> the God of Jacob does not perceive." (94:7)

Against this, the psalms consistently assert that God does see, God does hear, God does perceive, and God does act. The psalms maintain, again and again, that God is an active agent in the world. God answers prayers. God is at work, guiding history toward a final chapter that God has authored. At times this means that God intervenes in history in order to accomplish what the psalms often call God's "wondrous works." At times the Lord heals diseases and provides escape from oppressors. God often intervenes to topple and upset the upside-down structures of human hierarchy, which so often serve only to make the rich richer, the poor poorer, and the oppressors more powerful:

> [The LORD is the one] who executes justice for the oppressed;
> who gives food to the hungry.
>
> The LORD sets the prisoners free;
> the LORD opens the eyes of the blind.
> The LORD lifts up those who are bowed down;
> the LORD loves the righteous.
> The LORD watches over the strangers;
> he upholds the orphan and the widow,
> but the way of the wicked he brings to ruin. (146:7–9)

But God's activity in the world is not always disruptive. God's interventions are not always in the midst of crisis for the purpose of making a major course correction. The psalms also affirm activities such as *blessing, forgiving,* and *covenant keeping* are actions that God regularly takes. God's blessing activities are powerful actions whereby God grants divine power to another party *for the sake of life.* The psalms affirm that where God's blessing occurs, life thrives (see Ps. 134). It is consistent with God's very nature that God blesses, and thus the creation teems with life: a new generation is born, harvests are bountiful, joy replaces sadness, people find purpose and meaning. In a similar way, God's forgiveness is the act whereby God removes the stain of sin that curbs the vitality of creation. Forgiveness is often portrayed solely in a negative way, as the forgetting of a crime or as the covering up of a mark. But forgiveness is a far more active type of thing. In forgiveness, God reknits a relationship that has been torn in half. God restores community and thus provides a means by which relationships can thrive. Finally, when God keeps the promises of the covenants that God has made, God maintains the divine relationship with the people of Israel (including individual members of Israel) and with creation (including individual aspects of creation). According to the psalms, the covenant relationships are grounded in God's free choice of Israel (and of creation) and in God's loving faithfulness, which includes God's unequivocal and enduring commitment to the relationship. Psalm 145 captures the scope of God's covenantal commitment and loving faithfulness as clearly and as eloquently as any passage in the Psalter:

> The LORD is gracious and merciful,
>     slow to anger and abounding in steadfast love.
> The LORD is good to all,
>     and his compassion is over all that he has made.
>
> . . . . . . . . . . . . . . . . . . . . . . . . . . . . . . . . . . . . . . . . . . . .
>
> The LORD is faithful in all his words,
>     and gracious in all his deeds.
> The LORD upholds all who are falling,
>     and raises up all who are bowed down.
> The eyes of all look to you,
>     and you give them their food in due season.
> You open your hand,
>     satisfying the desire of every living thing.
> The LORD is just in all his ways,
>     and kind in all his doings.
> The LORD is near to all who call on him,
>     to all who call on him in truth.
> He fulfills the desire of all who fear him;
>     he also hears their cry, and saves them. (vv. 8–9, 13b–19)

## Conclusion

As we wrote in the introduction to this volume, the psalms are the poetry of faith: they are not meant to be studied; they are meant to be read. The point of learning to read the psalms is not to analyze them—to "torture a confession" out of them, in the words of the poet Billy Collins. The point is rather to learn to surf on their crest, to sing from their mountaintops, to groan from their depths. This is true both about the psalms as a whole and about the theology of the psalms. The theology of the psalms is a *lived theology*. It is a theology that is less about figuring out all of the best answers to tricky questions and more about living out life with other broken people, in the midst of a broken world, and in relationship with a God of loving faithfulness.

---

**NOT WHAT THEY SAY, BUT WHAT THEY DO**

In this chapter we have argued in favor of thinking about the theology of the psalms in terms of what they say *about God*. A different way of approaching the topic of the theology of the psalms is to focus not on what they say but on *what they do*. Scholar Harry Nasuti has argued that what is truly important about the psalms is not just that they say things about God but rather that they give people the words to speak to God. In other words, what the psalms do is make a relationship with God possible because we take up the words of the psalms and speak them to God. Nasuti writes that "of at least equal importance for a theology of the psalms is an understanding of the way these texts make available a relationship between God and the believing individuals and communities that have used them." And again, "One of the most distinctive aspects of the psalms is their ability to mediate a divine-human encounter through their continued use as first-person speech by praying individuals. By enabling the praying individual to assume the correct stance before God, these psalms help to make available an experience of God."[a]

a. Harry Nasuti, "God at Work in the Word," in *Soundings in the Theology of the Psalms*, ed. Rolf A. Jacobson (Minneapolis: Fortress, 2011), 29, 40.

---

Along those lines, it is not an accident that the book of Psalms ends with a psalm that is nothing more than an extended call for everyone to join Israel's song of praise—an invitation for all creation to join in the praying, singing, groaning, teaching way of living the theology of the psalms. The Psalter ends with an invitation:

> [1] Praise the LORD!
> Praise God in his sanctuary;
>     praise him in his mighty firmament!
> [2] Praise him for his mighty deeds;
>     praise him according to his surpassing greatness!
>
> [3] Praise him with trumpet sound;
>     praise him with lute and harp!
> [4] Praise him with tambourine and dance;
>     praise him with strings and pipe!
> [5] Praise him with clanging cymbals;
>     praise him with loud clashing cymbals!
> [6] Let everything that breathes praise the LORD!
> Praise the LORD! (Ps. 150)

## GOING DEEPER

To increase your understanding of the concepts introduced in this chapter, consider doing one or more of the following exercises:

1. Open up a Bible and find the psalms. Read until you have found ten images for God. Draw the ten images on one page.
2. Find a friend who has not studied the psalms and explain the concept that "God does not mind being questioned or even challenged" to them in words that they can understand. Ask them for their response to the concept.
3. This chapter has argued that the dominant theological message of the psalms is "The Lord is a God of loving faithfulness." Write a psalm in which you either argue against this concept or give thanks by using its words.

## FOR FURTHER READING

Brueggemann, Walter. *Israel's Praise: Doxology against Idolatry and Ideology.* Minneapolis: Fortress, 1988.

Jacobson, Rolf A. "Christian Theology of the Psalms." In *The Oxford Handbook on the Psalms*, ed. William P. Brown, 499–512. Oxford: Oxford University Press, 2014.

———, ed. *Soundings in the Theology of the Psalms: Perspectives and Methods in Contemporary Scholarship.* Minneapolis: Fortress, 2011.

Kraus, Hans-Joachim. *Theology of the Psalms.* Minneapolis: Augsburg, 1986.

Miller, Patrick. *They Cried to the Lord: The Form and Theology of Biblical Prayer.* Minneapolis: Fortress, 1994.

# Scripture Index

# Subject Index

acrostic poems, 15, 96
affliction. *See* enemies; suffering
African Americans, 107
Akinsiku, Ajinbayo, 115
alienation, 71, 97, 120
anointing, 134
Anselm, 162
Asaph, 28, 87–88, 105, 145–46
audience, 38–39, 44, 52–54
Auffret, Pierre, 159

Babylon, 99–101, 137. *See also* exile
blessing, 22, 136, 157, 183
Brown, William, 49–50, 114n3, 148–49, 159,
    161, 175
Broyles, Craig, 137
Brueggemann, Walter, 26, 154, 166, 170

call to praise, 44–45
canonical interpretation, 141–42
celebration, 104, 109. *See also* festivals
challenging God, 179
chaos, 13, 168, 169n8
chiasm, 96–97, 159
Christ, 64, 95. *See also* messianic expectations
Ciardi, John, 1, 2, 32
Clifford, Richard, 74
Collins, Billy, 2–3
communication, and structure, 19
community, 39, 40–44, 47, 53, 56, 179
complaint language, of lament psalms, 39–41
confidence. *See* psalms of trust; trust

content, and genre, 36
context, importance of, 31–32, 35
covenant
with Abraham and Sarah, 170
with David, 147, 150–52, 155
with Israel, 166, 183–84
and psalmist, 96–97
"covering" the psalms, 95
creation, 74, 65, 168–69, 178–79
creation psalms, 70–74, 72n15
crisis, 38, 47–48, 54–55, 172, 176. *See also*
    suffering

Davage, David (neé Willgren), 156
David, 33, 63–64, 74–76, 79, 86, 126. *See also*
    covenant: with David; Psalter: final form
    and shaping; superscriptions of psalms
deClaissé-Walford, Nancy, 154
doubt, 173

Edomites, 101
Egyptian Hallel, 156. *See also* festivals
enemies, 96–98, 134
enthronement psalms, 64–66, 153
Ethan, 28, 87
evildoers. *See* wicked(ness)
exile, 63, 101, 144. *See also* Babylon
exodus, 74, 104
expression, poetry as, 2
extending metaphors, 16–19
Ezrahites, 87